Performance Tasks and Rubrics for Middle School Mathematics

Performance tasks are highly effective tools to assist you in implementing rigorous standards. But how do you create, evaluate, and use such tools? In this bestselling book, educational experts Charlotte Danielson and Elizabeth Marquez explain how to construct and apply performance tasks to gauge students' deeper understanding of mathematical concepts at the middle school level. You'll learn how to:

- Evaluate the quality of performance tasks, whether you've written them yourself or found them online;
- Use performance tasks for instructional decision-making and to prepare students for summative assessments;
- Create your own performance tasks, or adapt pre-made tasks to best suit students' needs;
- Design and use scoring rubrics to evaluate complex performance tasks;
- Use your students' results to communicate more effectively with parents.

This must-have second edition is fully aligned to the Common Core State Standards and assessments and includes a variety of new performance tasks and rubrics, along with samples of student work. Additionally, downloadable student handout versions of all the performance tasks are available as free eResources from our website (www.routledge.com/9781138906914), so you can easily distribute them to your class.

Charlotte Danielson is an educational consultant now based in San Francisco, California. She has taught at all levels from kindergarten through college, and has worked as an administrator, a curriculum director, and a staff developer.

Elizabeth (Liz) Marquez is a mathematics assessment specialist at Educational Testing Service. She has taught mathematics in both middle and high school. Liz is a recipient of the Presidential Award for Excellence in Mathematics Teaching and the Princeton University Prize for Distinguished Secondary School Teaching.

Math Performance Tasks

Performance Tasks and Rubrics for Early Elementary Mathematics:
Meeting Rigorous Standards and Assessments
Charlotte Danielson and Pia Hansen

Performance Tasks and Rubrics for Upper Elementary Mathematics:
Meeting Rigorous Standards and Assessments
Charlotte Danielson and Joshua Dragoon

Performance Tasks and Rubrics for Middle School Mathematics:
Meeting Rigorous Standards and Assessments
Charlotte Danielson and Elizabeth Marquez

Performance Tasks and Rubrics for High School Mathematics:
Meeting Rigorous Standards and Assessments
Charlotte Danielson and Elizabeth Marquez

Performance Tasks and Rubrics for Middle School Mathematics

Meeting Rigorous Standards and Assessments

Second Edition

Charlotte Danielson and Elizabeth Marquez

NEW YORK AND LONDON

Second edition published 2016
by Routledge
711 Third Avenue, New York, NY 10017

and by Routledge
2 Park Square, Milton Park, Abingdon, Oxon, OX14 4RN

Routledge is an imprint of the Taylor & Francis Group, an informa business

© 2016 Taylor & Francis

The right of Charlotte Danielson and Elizabeth Marquez to be identified as authors of this work has been asserted by them in accordance with sections 77 and 78 of the Copyright, Designs and Patents Act 1988.

All rights reserved. No part of this book may be reprinted or reproduced or utilised in any form or by any electronic, mechanical, or other means, now known or hereafter invented, including photocopying and recording, or in any information storage or retrieval system, without permission in writing from the publishers.

Trademark notice: Product or corporate names may be trademarks or registered trademarks, and are used only for identification and explanation without intent to infringe.

First edition published by Routledge 1997

Library of Congress Cataloging in Publication Data
Names: Danielson, Charlotte. | Marquez, Elizabeth.
Title: Performance tasks and rubrics for middle school mathematics : meeting
     rigorous standards and assessments / by Charlotte Danielson and Elizabeth
     Marquez.
Description: Second edition. | New York : Routledge, 2016.
Identifiers: LCCN 2015037983 | ISBN 9781138906914 (pbk.) |
     ISBN 9781315695297 (e-book)
Subjects: LCSH: Mathematics—Study and teaching (Middle school)—Evaluation.
Classification: LCC QA11 .D3454 2016 | DDC 510.71/2—dc23
LC record available at http://lccn.loc.gov/2015037983

ISBN: 978-1-138-90691-4 (pbk)
ISBN: 978-1-315-69529-7 (ebk)

Typeset in Palatino
by Swales & Willis Ltd, Exeter, Devon, UK

To Brian and Katie

Contents

eResources viii
Meet the Authors ix
Foreword by Jay McTighe xi
Preface xiii
Acknowledgments xvi

1 **Introduction: What Is Performance Assessment?** 1

2 **Why Use Performance Assessment?** 10

3 **Making an Evaluation Plan** 19

4 **Understanding Quality Performance Tasks** 27

5 **Creating and Adapting Performance Tasks** 34

6 **Using Rubrics to Evaluate Complex Performance** 42

7 **Creating and Adapting Rubrics** 56

8 **Middle School Mathematics Performance Tasks** 69

eResources

The student handouts that accompany the tasks in this book are available on our website as free eResources, so you can download and print them for classroom use. You can access the eResources by visiting the book product page on our website: www.routledge.com/9781138906914. Click on the tab that says "eResources" and select the files. They will begin downloading to your computer.

Meet the Authors

Charlotte Danielson is an internationally recognized expert specializing recently in the area of teacher effectiveness, focusing on the design of teacher evaluation systems that both ensure teacher quality and promote professional learning.

Charlotte began her career as an economist but soon realized her passion for education. She became a teacher and later worked as a curriculum director, staff developer, and instructional coach, and then later as an advisor on educational policy. Her work in classroom-based assessment—in particular in the design and interpretation of performance tasks—served as a prototype for her later work in the analysis of teacher performance.

After years in the classroom, Charlotte realized that clear standards of practice were essential to advancing the profession. She wrote the *Framework for Teaching*, initially published in 1996 and intended to define good practice, primarily to inform professional learning and only later used as a tool for teacher evaluation. As such, it has, in many places, transformed school culture. She then began advising school districts, states, and countries on how to incorporate principles of professional learning into their evaluation systems.

Charlotte currently advises State Education Departments and National Ministries and Departments of Education, both in the United States and overseas. She is a sought-after keynote speaker at national and international conferences, and a policy consultant to legislative and administrative bodies. She continues to base her work on a profound awareness of the complexity of teaching, the nature of learning, and the need to work to advance the professionalism of teaching.

Elizabeth (Liz) Marquez is a mathematics assessment specialist at Educational Testing Service (ETS), where she develops performance tasks, both formative and summative, as part of the Cognitively Based Assessment of, for, and as Learning (CBAL) research project. Much of Liz's work at ETS has addressed how the use of performance assessments along with learning progressions can improve classroom teaching and learning so that assessment strengthens instruction rather than displacing it. In addition to assessments, Liz has developed teacher support materials and has delivered workshops using those materials throughout the United States.

Liz's previous work at ETS includes development of the National Board for Professional Teaching Standards (NBPTS) certificates for both middle and high school mathematics teachers.

Prior to joining ETS, Liz taught mathematics in grades 7–12. She is a recipient of the Presidential Award for Excellence in Mathematics Teaching and the Princeton University Prize for Distinguished Secondary School Teaching. Liz's classroom was featured in films on the art of teaching and on standards-based instruction. She has co-authored articles, research papers, and books on teaching, learning, and assessment in mathematics education.

Foreword

In June of 2010, the National Governors Association (NGA) and the Council Chief State School Officers (CCSSO) released the Common Core State Standards for Mathematics. The release of this set of "next generation" standards has profoundly influenced the vision and practice of mathematics education throughout the nation. In specifying the content of mathematics to be taught across the grades, the CCSS for Mathematics stress conceptual understanding along with procedural skill. These new standards have introduced eight Standards for Mathematical Practice to highlight the importance of thinking mathematically and applying mathematical reasoning to address real world issues and problems. Many states have adopted the Common Core mathematics standards directly, while others have revised their previous mathematics standards to be more closely aligned with the CCSS.

Through its call for a greater emphasis on problem solving, reasoning, and mathematical communication, these new core standards unambiguously support the expanded use of performance tasks for classroom instruction and assessment. Indeed, effective performance tasks call for the Mathematical Practices by engaging students in applying mathematical concepts and ways of thinking in the context of tackling "authentic" problems.

While the emphases of these new core standards are clear, a number of practical questions remain: How do teachers develop "authentic" tasks to assess students' understanding and mathematical reasoning? How does the use of performance tasks fit with more traditional forms of assessment in mathematics? How do teachers evaluate student responses since performance tasks typically call for more than a single, correct answer?

Charlotte Danielson and Elizabeth Marquez offer timely and practical answers in this readable guide to the development and use of performance tasks and rubrics in middle school classrooms. The book provides an excellent overview of the rationale for, and the strengths and limitations of, the use of performance tasks to assess student achievement and progress in mathematics. They offer a user-friendly, field-tested process for developing performance tasks and rubrics, along with practical advice for evaluating student work, selecting "anchors," and establishing performance standards. Finally, the sample tasks, rubrics and student work samples provide tried and true resources for immediate use, while serving as models to guide development of additional tasks and scoring tools.

xii ◆ Foreword

Readers of *Performance Tasks and Rubrics for Middle School Mathematics* will not be confronted with an ivory tower treatise on what should be. Rather, they will discover a valuable resource, grounded in the wisdom of years of experience in schools and classrooms, for making the vision of the new core standards come to life.

Jay McTighe
Educational Author and Consultant

Preface

Educators have long recognized the unique role and importance of assessment in the classroom environment. Assessment provides valuable information for both teachers and students regarding how well everyone is doing. Students can see where they went wrong in their understanding, and teachers can determine whether a concept needs to be re-taught or whether it should be taught differently. This function, of monitoring progress on important learning goals, is the first and most important purpose of assessment.

Assessment also defines what students must know and be able to do to succeed in a particular teacher's class. Students frequently say that they don't know, until they have seen a teacher's first tests in the fall, just what she values. Is she a stickler for details? Or are the big ideas all that is important? What teachers assess and how they assess it convey what is important, both to them and in the subject. This can serve a clarifying purpose for teachers as well as students. By specifying what their students should study and determining how best to elicit evidence of how well they know it, teachers make decisions about what is truly important. Through the assessments teachers design and the feedback they provide to students, teachers reveal, both explicitly and implicitly, their understanding of and beliefs about curriculum and standards.

Since the release of the first edition of this book the educational landscape has changed enormously. The No Child Left Behind Act (NCLB) mandated annual testing and performance targets for subgroups of students. Race to the Top led to shifts in teacher evaluation, promoted the adoption of the Common Core State Standards, and led to the creation of the PARCC and Smarter Balanced assessment consortia. When tests "count," they motivate as well. That is, to the extent that tests or other assessments are used to calculate students' grades, students will try to do well. Teachers are also held accountable for student performance on standardized tests and other measures of achievement as a result of the changes to teacher evaluation in recent years. Some states and school districts use test scores as the basis for rewards or sanctions. In whatever ways test scores matter, teachers want their students to do well. Most teachers will provide instruction that supports their students' success on these tests, especially when stakes are high.

Tests and other assessments influence practice by defining important content. But the form of an assessment matters as well. That is, when students are asked on tests (and know in advance that they will be asked) to answer a number of multiple-choice or short-answer questions, they tend to prepare in that manner, committing to memory that which they predict will be on the test. If deeper understanding is not required for the test, they may not strive to achieve it. If a question is ambiguous, they will seek to "read the mind" of the teacher, to determine the right answer even if they believe another is better. The form of assessment also affects teachers' practices. If a test does not require, or does not reward, understanding, why should teachers emphasize it in their own classrooms, particularly since it typically requires more instructional time than rote teaching? If all that is needed in mathematics, for example, is for students to get the right answer (possibly without understanding why the procedure works) then the procedure is all that will be provided in some classrooms.

However, if assessment is designed to gauge deeper understanding, students will work to show what they know, even if they are unable to reach a single, correct answer. In contrast with multiple-choice questions that comprise the bulk of most large-scale, standardized tests, the heart of the assessment practices espoused in this text reflect the belief that learning isn't an all-or-nothing proposition. Assessment has the power to reveal where along a trajectory of learning a student currently is so that he or she may be supported in moving further along that trajectory. And assessments can reveal important things about students' understandings and their misconceptions. Assessments matter, therefore, both in what they assess and how they assess it. The content of a test affects what students study and teachers teach, and the form of the assessment affects how they approach the task. Teachers have discovered, for example, that if they want their students to become better writers, they must make good writing count in the classroom; they must teach it systematically and assess it authentically. A test of correcting errors, for example, will not do; they must assess students' actual writing. Similarly, if teachers want students to acquire skills in solving mathematical problems, or communicating their mathematical ideas, they must both teach and assess those skills.

These considerations have provided much of the energy behind the movement towards "performance assessment," that is, students actually creating or constructing an answer to a question. Teachers and policy-makers alike have discovered that when assessment tasks more accurately mirror the types of learning goals they have for students—both in the content and the form of assessment—the learning environment is transformed. The assessments themselves tend to be motivational and engaging: students invest energy in the tasks and commit to them. In addition, performance assessments even serve to educate as well as assess student learning. Students learn from doing performance tasks.

However, performance assessment has one enormous drawback: it is time-consuming to do, both to design and to work into classroom instructional time. Even teachers who are committed to the practice of performance assessment find that they don't have time to design good performance tasks, to try them out with students, and perfect them for later use. Furthermore, most teachers have only limited experience designing performance tasks and scoring rubrics as part of their professional preparation. And even when educators have learned such skills as part of their continuing professional growth, they may lack the confidence to use such performance tasks as a central part of their assessment plan.

This book is designed to address this need. It is based on the assumption that many educators are interested in incorporating performance assessment into their classroom routines, but have either not yet acquired the technical skill or do not have the time required to design them on their own. This book provides a collection of performance tasks and scoring rubrics for a number of topics in middle school mathematics, which teachers can use as is, or adapt for their students and their particular situation. It is intended to save time for busy educators, to provide examples of tested performance tasks. The samples of student work provide a range of responses, to clarify the tasks, and to anchor the points on the scoring rubrics.

Chapter 1 provides the reader with an introduction to performance assessment and how it is distinguished from traditional testing. Chapter 2 offers a rationale for performance assessment, explaining its strengths (and its drawbacks) as compared with more traditional approaches. In Chapter 3 the reader can find guidance in making an evaluation plan, and linking that plan to the overall approach to curriculum development. Chapter 4 shares criteria for quality performance tasks. Chapter 5 offers a step-by-step procedure for creating and adapting a performance task for classroom use, and Chapter 6 provides an overview of how scoring rubrics can be used to evaluate complex performance. In Chapter 7, a process for the design and adaptation of rubrics is shared. Chapter 8 is the heart of the collection, and offers performance tasks (some with samples of student work) and rubrics, covering the major topics in middle school mathematics, designed to be adapted, or used as is, in your classroom. The Routledge website, www.routledge.com/9781138906914, contains student handouts for of each of the 24 tasks so that you may print and distribute them to students.

Acknowledgments

The authors would like to thank Leslie Abrutyn, Assistant Superintendent of the Penn Delco School District in Aston, Pennsylvania, for initiating the project that resulted in this book. Thanks are also due to Barbara Smith, Mathematics Supervisor of the Unionville-Chadds Ford School District and Donna Bucci of the Penn Delco Schcol District.

The authors would also like to acknowledge Richard North, Mary LoScalzo, and Dino Ippolito of Hommocks Middle School of Larchmont, New York, for contributing student work samples.

The authors would like to thank Mark Lewis Wagner (www.drawingonearth. org) for providing the photographs of a chalk drawing done at the Alameda Naval Air Station in June 2008.

Special thanks are also due to Bena Kallick for granting permission for reprinting several of the tasks (with their accompanying student work) from Exemplars, RR 1, PO Box 7390, Underhill, VT 05489.

The authors acknowledge with special appreciation the extensive amount of guidance, encouragement, and editorial insight provided by Lauren Davis, Senior Editor in Education at Routledge. She helped us make the revisions necessary to make the books in this series current, relevant, and useful to teachers.

We would also like to thank Jay McTighe for his thoughtful Foreword, as well as the reviewers who looked at the first edition and made suggestions for updates.

1

Introduction

What Is Performance Assessment?

This book concerns the classroom use of performance assessment, and the evaluation of student work in response to performance tasks. It contains a collection of performance tasks in middle school mathematics, but also includes guidance for educators to design or adapt performance tasks for their own use and to be a wise consumer of performance tasks that may be available to them.

While performance assessment is essential to a well-rounded assessment plan, it should not be used exclusively. Other item types associated with traditional testing have an important role to play, particularly in assessing a large domain or evaluating student knowledge. But in assessing student understanding, in order to ascertain how well students can apply their knowledge, some type of performance assessment is essential.

In this book, performance assessment means any assessment of student learning that requires the evaluation of student writing, products, or behavior. That is, it includes all assessment with the exception of multiple choice, matching, true/false testing, or problems with a single correct answer. Classroom-based performance assessment includes all such assessment that occurs in the classroom for formative or summative purposes and is evaluated by teachers as distinct from large-scale, state-wide testing programs.

Performance assessment is fundamentally criterion-referenced rather than norm-referenced. That is, teachers who adopt performance assessment are concerned with the degree to which students can demonstrate knowledge and skill in a certain field. They know what it means to demonstrate competence; the purpose of a performance assessment is to allow students to show what they can do. The criteria for evaluating performance are important; teachers use their professional judgment in establishing such criteria and defining levels of performance. And the standards they set for student performance are typically above those expected for minimal competency; they define accomplished performance.

Norm-referenced tests are less valuable to teachers than are performance assessments. True, teachers may learn what their students can do compared to other students of the same age. However, the items on the test may or may not reflect the curriculum of a given school or district; to the extent that these are different, the information provided may not be of value to the teacher. Moreover, the results of most standardized tests are not known for some time. Even for those items included in a school's curriculum, it does not help a teacher to know in June that a student did not know, in April, a concept that was taught the previous November. Of what possible use is that information to the teacher in June? It may not even still be true. And even if true, the information comes too late to be useful.

In addition, the only way students demonstrate progress on a norm-referenced test is in comparison to other students. Progress per se is not shown as progress. That is, a student's standing may move from the 48th percentile to the 53rd percentile. However, the student may not have learned much but other students may have learned less! So while norm-referenced tests have their value, for example for large-scale program evaluation, they are of limited use to teachers who want to know what each of their students have learned with respect to the Common Core State Standards or any set of standards that guides their curriculum. Performance assessment, then, is criterion-referenced. It reflects the curriculum goals of a teacher, school, or district with respect to the set of standards that guides their curriculum and when used in the context of classroom teaching, it informs instructional decisions.

The remaining sections of this chapter describe the different uses and types of performance assessment.

The Uses of Classroom-Based Performance Assessment

Assessment of student learning in the classroom is done for many purposes and can serve many ends. When teachers design or choose their assessment strategies, it is helpful to determine, at the outset, which of the many possible uses they have in mind. Some possibilities are described here.

Instructional Decision-Making

Many teachers discover, after they have taught a concept, that many students didn't "get it"; that, while they may have had looks of understanding on their faces, and may have participated in the instructional activities, they are unable to demonstrate the knowledge or understanding on their own.

This is important information for teachers to have, as they determine what to do next with a class, or even with a few students. They may decide that they must re-teach the concept, or create a different type of instructional activity. Alternatively, if only a few students lack understanding, a teacher might decide to work with them separately, or to design an activity that can be used for peer tutoring.

Whatever course of action a teacher decides upon, however, it is decided on the basis of information regarding student understanding. That implies that the assessment strategies used will reveal student understanding, or lack of it. When used for instructional decision-making, it is the teacher alone who uses the information to determine whether the instructional activities achieved their intended purpose.

Feedback to Students

Performance assessment, like any assessment, may also be used to provide feedback to students regarding their progress. Depending on how it is constructed, a performance task can let students know in which dimensions of performance they excel, and in which they need to devote additional energy. Such feedback is, by its nature, individualized; the feedback provided to one student will be very different from that provided to another if their performances are different. It is efficient for the teacher, however, since the important dimensions of performance have been identified beforehand.

Communication with Families

Actual student performance on well-designed tasks can provide families with authentic evidence of their child's level of functioning. Many parents are skeptical of tests that they don't understand, and are not sure of the meaning of numbers, percentiles and scaled scores. But student answers to an open-ended question or to other performance assessments are easy to understand and can serve to demonstrate to families the level of understanding of their child. These samples of student work are highly beneficial for open house or parent conferences, serving to educate parents and to validate the judgments of the teacher.

Such indication of student performance is of particular importance if a teacher is concerned about a child and wants to persuade a parent/guardian that action is needed. It is impossible for parents, when confronted with the work of their own child, to question the commitment of the teacher in meeting that child's needs. Whether the work is exemplary and the teacher is recommending a more advanced placement, or the work reveals little understanding, the actual samples of student performance are invaluable to a teacher in making a case for action.

Summative Evaluation of Student Learning

In addition to having formative purposes, a performance assessment may be used to evaluate student learning and may contribute to decisions regarding grades. The issue of grading is complex and will be addressed more fully on page 17 of this book, but the results from performance tasks, like any assessment, can serve to substantiate a teacher's judgment in assigning a grade.

Different Types of Classroom-Based Assessment

Assessment takes many forms, depending on the types of instructional goals being assessed, and the use to which the assessment will be put. The major types are presented in table form (Table 1.1), and are described in the following sections.

Summative Assessments

Summative assessments have always been (and will continue to be) an important method for ascertaining what students know and can do.

When teachers decide to move to more authentic aspects of performance in order to evaluate student learning, they do not necessarily abandon traditional types of summative assessments. On the contrary, they may use traditional tests or item types for that which they are well suited (for example, for sampling knowledge), recognizing their substantial strengths as a methodology. However, when teachers want to measure the depth, rigor, and complexity of comprehension they may use summative assessments which include performance tasks or technology-enhanced items or extended constructed-response items. Of course, summative as well as formative assessments may include both traditional and non-traditional item types.

Summative assessments are generally given to students under what we call "testing conditions," that is, conditions that ensure that we are actually getting the authentic work of individuals and that the experience is the same for all students. Testing conditions are:

- *Limited time.* Generally speaking, time for a test is strictly limited. Students must complete the test within a certain amount of time (frequently a class period, but sometimes more or less than that). This provision ensures that some students don't devote far greater time to the assignments than others.
- *Limited (or no) resources.* Although there are exceptions to this rule (such as open-book tests and the use of calculators), students taking a test are usually not permitted to consult materials as they work. An insistence on no additional resources rules out, of course, trips to the library while taking a test. This provision ensures that what students produce on the test reflects only their own understanding.
- *No talking with peers or looking at others' papers.* When taking a test, it is important that students produce their own work. Unless teachers adhere to this condition, they are never sure whether what they receive from an individual student reflects that student's understanding, or that of his or her friends.

Table 1.1 Forms of Classroom-Based Assessment

Assessment Types	
Formative: Both formal and informal ongoing assessment of student learning that provides evidence used by teachers to adjust instruction and by students to improve their learning. When informal, it allows for observation of spontaneous behavior.	*Summative*: Formal assessment given periodically to determine what students know and can do with respect to some standard or benchmark, e.g., end-of-unit test, midterm exam, final project.
Item Types (may appear on a formative or a summative assessment)	
Traditional items (may appear on a formative or a summative assessment)	*Non-traditional items** (may appear on a formative or a summative assessment) Results in a physical or written product and allows for observation of structured or spontaneous behavior
• Selected response: multiple choice, matching, and true/false questions • Fill in the blanks • Solve without showing the process • Short constructed response	• Performance tasks • Extended constructed response • Technology-enhanced

Note: *For the purposes of this book, extended constructed response and all non-traditional assessment is considered performance assessment.

In addition, summative assessments are traditionally of two basic types: selected response and constructed response.

- ◆ *Selected response.* In a selected-response test, students select the best answer from those given. True/false and matching tests may also be included in this category. Short-answer items are technically constructed-response items (since the student supplies the answer), but since there is generally a single right answer, such items are a special case, and share more characteristics in their scoring with multiple-choice items.
- ◆ *Constructed response.* In a constructed-response test, students answer a question in their own words. Open-ended questions are constructed response, as are essay questions on a test.

Of course, a single summative assessment may contain a combination of selected-response and constructed-response items. In fact, most tests do: they generally consist of some multiple-choice, true/false, short-answer, or matching items for a portion of the test and several constructed-response items for the remainder. The balance between these different types of test items varies enormously, by subject, grade level, and the preference of the teacher.

Formative Assessments

Unlike summative assessments, formative assessments are an ongoing part of the instructional process in which evidence is collected either formally or informally of student engagement with mathematical concepts, skills, and processes. As incorporated into classroom practice, formative assessment provides teachers with evidence of student understanding that can they can use to determine next steps in instruction in a timely fashion. For example, if teachers observe student behavior that reveals a misconception, they can make an on-the-spot intervention, or if a teacher gathers evidence through a formal classroom assessment the results of that assessment can be determined within a day or two with appropriate interventions taken.

Performance assessment is most often associated with formative assessment but performance assessment such as extended constructed-response items are increasingly becoming part of classroom-based and standardized summative assessments.

Product

A product is any item produced by students which is evaluated according to established criteria and can be the result of either a formative or summative

> ### ☑ Professional Development Tip
>
> **Focus on Formative Assessment**
>
> Identification and discussion of types of formative assessments, both formal and informal, can be helpful to teachers. For instance, just knowing that formative assessment can be as simple as a check for understanding or as complex as analysis of a test in order to determine the level at which a student is progressing in their understanding of mathematics. Having teachers demonstrate the specific ways that they check for understanding or analyze test results or use assessment results to determine next steps in instruction can be of great help to other teachers. For instance, it can help a teacher understand the most effective way to check for understanding—e.g., nodding heads to indicate understanding versus using exit tickets to find out what students know. Examining the differences between summative and formative assessment is also a useful exercise. For instance, it is important to understand that if the results of an assessment, no matter how small, are not used to inform instruction, it cannot be formative.

performance assessment. A product is a thing, a physical object, and is often (but not always) produced by students outside of school time. Students may take as long as they want and need to, and may consult books and speak with other people. Products may be one of two types: written or physical.

- *Written products.* A written product may be a term paper, an essay for homework, a journal entry, a drama, or a lab report. It is anything written by students, but not under testing conditions.
- *Physical products.* A physical product may be, for example, a diorama, a science construction, a project in industrial arts, a sculpture, or a 3D copy. Physical products are three-dimensional things, and take up space.

Some projects done by students represent a combination of written and physical products. For example, most science fair projects consist of a physical construction of some sort, combined with a written description of the scientific principles involved.

Products are a rich source of information for teachers in seeking to understand what their students know and can do. However, they have two significant disadvantages, which limit their usefulness for high-stakes assessment. The first relates to authenticity. When a student turns in a project, the teacher has no way of knowing the degree to which the work reflects the student's own knowledge and understanding, and the degree to which the student's parents or others might have assisted. The second disadvantage is that while a product may enable students to demonstrate depth of under-standing, they don't accomplish what most assessments must do, namely to sample the breadth of knowledge and skill.

For instructional purposes, most teachers encourage their students to obtain as much help as they can get; students are bound to learn more from an assignment with the insights of additional people. However, for purposes of assessment we need to know what each student can do; this requirement limits the usefulness of out-of-class assignments for evaluation. When used, they should be supplemented by other sources of information (for example, an assignment given under testing conditions) of which the teacher can be sure of authorship.

Behavior

Lastly, students demonstrate their knowledge or skill through their behavior, and this behavior can be evaluated. Behavior is that aspect of student performance which does not result in a tangible object; once completed, it is finished. However, behavior may be captured and stored, and then evaluated and as such can be the result of either a formative or summative performance assessment. For example, a skit may be video recorded, or a student reading aloud may be audio recorded. There are two types of behavior that may be used for evaluation:

- ◆ *Structured behavior.* In structured behavior, students are performing according to a pre-established framework. They may be staging a debate or a panel discussion. They may be giving a skit, performing a dance, or making a presentation. Teachers may be interviewing their students. Drama and speech classes depend on this type of performance to evaluate learning; it is useful in other fields as well. In virtually every state, acquiring a driver's license depends on successful performance behind the wheel, and assessments in world languages typically include a spoken portion.
- ◆ *Spontaneous behavior.* Students can also reveal their understanding through their spontaneous behavior. For example, their interaction when working on group projects, their questions during a discussion and their choices during free time, all demonstrate important aspects of their learning.

Because of the unstructured nature of spontaneous behavior, it is useful primarily as a supplemental form of assessment. However, for certain types of instructional goals, such as skill in collaboration, it may be the only appropriate form. The documentation of spontaneous behavior depends on careful observation. Many teachers use checklists so they can make their "kid watching" as systematic as possible. Spontaneous behavior is most often associated with formative assessment.

Chapter Summary

◆ Classroom-based performance assessment is criterion-referenced and is used to evaluate student learning on clearly identified instructional goals with respect to the Common Core State Standards or any set of standards that guides their curriculum. As such, it should be designed to be of optimal usefulness to its different audiences: teachers, students, and parents.

◆ Classroom-based assessment may be used for several different purposes. An overall assessment plan will take all desired purposes into account.

◆ There are different types of classroom assessment. The major types are formative assessments and summative assessments either of which can include performance assessments resulting in various products and behavior. Depending on the types of instructional goals to be assessed, they are all valuable. For the purposes of this book all assessment except selected-response assessments are considered performance assessment.

2

Why Use Performance Assessment?

It is clear that the design and implementation of performance assessment are far more time-consuming than the use of traditional tests. Why, one might ask, should a busy educator go to the trouble of changing? A good question, and one that deserves a thoughtful answer.

First, it should be made clear that when teachers use performance assessment, they don't stop using traditional forms of assessment. Traditional forms of assessments will always be with us, and they should be. It is frequently important to ascertain what students know about a subject; alternatively, we must be sure that they have read an assignment. There is no substitute for a traditional type of quiz or test to ascertain these things. But as a steady diet, traditional assessments have serious limitations. These are described below.

The Limitations of Traditional Testing

When we refer to "traditional testing" in this book, we mean multiple-choice, true/false, matching, or short-answer assessments that teachers create or adapt for use in their classrooms. These are generally provided by the publishers of text programs, or have evolved over time. As noted above, they are useful for certain purposes (and they are certainly efficient to score), but when used exclusively, they have a negative influence.

Validity

The most serious criticism of traditional testing is that the range of student knowledge and skill that can be tested is extremely limited. Many aspects of understanding to which teachers and their communities are most committed simply don't lend themselves to multiple-choice assessment. To illustrate this point, it is helpful to identify the different categories of educational purposes (instructional goals) and to consider how they can be assessed.

There are, of course, many different ways to classify goals for this type of analysis; one comprehensive classification scheme is outlined below.

◆ *Knowledge.* Most types of knowledge, whether procedural knowledge (i.e., how to wash lab equipment), conceptual understanding (i.e., the meaning of slope), and the application of knowledge (i.e., determining the amount of paint needed to paint a room), may all be assessed through traditional means. Indeed, it is in the assessment of knowledge that traditional assessment rightfully exerts its strongest influence.

Conceptual understanding, however, is not ideally suited to traditional testing since students can memorize, for example, a definition of "slope" without really understanding it; their lack of understanding might not be revealed through a multiple-choice or matching test. It is only through their explanation of the concept in their own words, or their use of the concept in a problem that their understanding, or lack of it, is demonstrated.

◆ *Reasoning.* Traditional testing is poorly suited to the assessment of reasoning. While it is true that well-designed multiple-choice tests may be used to evaluate pure logic, most teachers without technical skills in this area are not advised to attempt it. Most of the reasoning we care about in schools (i.e., analyzing data, formulating and testing hypotheses, recognizing patterns) is better assessed through nontraditional means.

◆ *Communication.* In order to know whether students can communicate, we must ask them to do so in writing or speaking. Attempts are made, of course, to evaluate students' understanding of written text and spoken language through multiple-choice tests. To some extent these attempts are successful but they rarely give teachers information they did not already have through more informal means. For the productive aspects of communication writing and speaking—there is no substitute for students actually writing and speaking, and then evaluating their performance.

- *Skills*. Social skills and psychomotor skills are completely unsuited to traditional forms of assessment. A multiple-choice test on the rules of basketball does not tell a teacher whether or not a student can dribble the ball. And a matching test on how to work in groups does not convey whether students have actually acquired skills in collaboration. Nothing short of observation will do, using a carefully prepared observation guide. To the extent that skills are important aspects of learning, teachers must employ nontraditional assessment methods.
- *Affective Areas*. As with skills, traditional testing is entirely unsuited to the assessment of the affective domain. To the extent that teachers attempt to cultivate students' productive dispositions towards work (for example, habits of mind, reasoning and communication, attending to precision, and perseverance) they must look for little indicators through student behavior. As teachers try to cultivate mathematical practices in their students, like making sense of problems and persevering in solving them, they must look for little comments and signs from their students. Other aspects of the affective domain are equally ill-matched to traditional testing, from self-confidence, to traits such as honesty and respect for private property, through the ability to weigh ethical arguments. In short, life and career skills such as those as defined by the Partnership for 21st Century Skills are best assessed by non-traditional assessment.

As is evident from the descriptions above, if teachers use only traditional forms of assessment, they will be unable to assess many aspects (some would say the most important aspects) of student learning. Clearly, other methods such as constructed-response tests, projects, and behavior are needed. These alternative modes must therefore be designed and procedures developed for the evaluation of student work produced through these alternative means.

Design Issues

Measurement experts argue that most aspects of student knowledge and skill may be assessed through well-designed multiple-choice tests. They point to well-known tests that evaluate problem solving, reasoning, and data analysis. On further examination, by looking at the actual items, most teachers would probably agree that the items require some higher-level thinking on the part of students.

Teachers should not assume because such test items are possible to construct that they themselves can construct them, or should want to spend the necessary time to do so. These test items are designed by measurement experts and are extensively field-tested to ensure that they are both valid and reliable. Neither of these conditions is available to most practicing educators, who have their next day's lessons to think about.

When teachers try to design their own multiple-choice tests, they encounter three related, though somewhat distinct, difficulties:

- *Ambiguity.* A major challenge confronting test developers is to create multiple-choice test items in which the wrong answers are plausible and yet unambiguously wrong. Ideally, the distractors (the wrong answers) should be incorrect in ways in which students' thinking is typically flawed, so a student's pattern of wrong answers may reveal diagnostic information.

  Such tests are very difficult to construct. Most teachers have had the experience of creating a test in which students can, by guessing or using a process of elimination, determine the right answer even when they know very little about the subject.

- *Authenticity.* In order to engage students in meaningful work, it is helpful for assessment to be as authentic as possible. Students are more likely to produce work of good quality if the questions seem plausible and worthwhile. But to design an authentic multiple-choice test, one that elicits the desired knowledge and skill, is very difficult. Highly authentic questions tend to be long and cumbersome, while more focused questions are often found to be boring and inauthentic by students.

- *Time.* Good multiple-choice questions require a great deal of time to create. And unless they are tested before being used, teachers cannot be sure that they are valid. That is, the question may be ambiguous, or several of the choices may be plausible. Hence, students are justified in challenging such questions and the evaluations based on them.

These factors, taken together, suggest that teachers are unlikely to be successful in creating their own multiple-choice tests for complex learning. Experts in test design can succeed more often than novices, but even experts are limited in what is possible through the technique.

Influence on Instruction

Probably the most serious concern about the exclusive use of traditional testing relates to its effect on the instructional process. Since traditional tests are best suited to the assessment of low-level knowledge, such instructional goals are heavily represented (to the virtual exclusion of other, more complex, learning goals) in such tests. This is why some standardized tests are using performance assessment along with traditional assessment to determine what students know and can do with respect to a particular set of standards.

It is well known that "what you test is what you get." Through our assessment methods we convey to students what is important to learn. And when the tests we give reflect only factual or procedural knowledge, we signal to students that such knowledge is more important than their ability to reason, to solve problems, to work together collaboratively, or to write effectively. Since multiple-choice tests are best at evaluating students' command of factual knowledge, many students think that school learning is trivial, and never realize that their teachers value the expression of their own ideas, a creative approach to problems, or the design of an imaginative experiment.

The most powerful means teachers have at their disposal for shifting the culture of their classrooms to one of significant work is to change their assessment methodologies. While traditional tests will always have a value, combining their use with alternative means sends an important signal to students regarding what sort of learning is valued in school. If good ideas and imaginative projects count, students will begin to shift their conceptions of the meaning of school.

The Benefits of Performance Assessment

Many of the advantages of performance assessment are simply the reverse side of the limitations of traditional testing, namely, that they enable teachers to assess students in all those aspects of learning they value, in particular, writing and speaking, reasoning and problem solving, psychomotor and social skills, and the entire affective domain. However, there are many other benefits to be derived as well. These are described in the following sections.

Clarity as to Criteria and Standards

When teachers use performance assessment, they discover that they must be extremely clear, both to themselves and to their students, as to the criteria they will use to evaluate student work, and the standard of performance they expect. For many teachers, this clarity is greater than that required for traditional testing, and requires that they give sustained thought to difficult questions such as, "What do I really want my students to be able to do?" and, "What is most important in this unit?" and, "How good is good enough?"

These questions, while some of the most important that teachers ever consider, tend to be obscured by the pressure of daily work, and the normal routines of life in schools. The design of performance assessment tasks puts them at the center. Most teachers find that, while the questions are difficult to answer, their entire instructional program is greatly strengthened as a result of the effort.

Professional Dialogue about Criteria and Standards

If teachers create their performance assessments together, they must decide together how they will evaluate student work and what their standards will be. These are not easy discussions, but most teachers find them to be extremely valuable.

Occasionally, teachers find that their criteria for problem solving, for example, are very different from one another. One teacher may believe that the process used is more important than whether or not the answer is correct. Another may believe the reverse. They must resolve their differences in designing a problem solving task if they are to evaluate student work together. On the other hand, they could agree to disagree, and each use his or her own procedure. But the conversation will have been valuable in isolating such a fundamental difference in approach.

Improved Student Work

Virtually all teachers report improved quality of student work when they begin using performance assessment. This is due, no doubt, to several factors:

- *Clarity as to criteria and standards*. Just as greater clarity in criteria and standards is valuable to teachers and contributes to professional dialogue, it is essential for students. When students know what is expected, they are far more likely to be able to produce it than if they do not.
- *Greater confidence in work*. When students understand the criteria and standards to be used in evaluating their work, they can approach it with greater confidence. The criteria provide them with guidelines for their work and they can estimate the time required to produce work of good quality. All this tends to increase student engagement and pride in their work.
- *High expectations*. When they make the standards for exemplary performance clear to students, teachers are sending an important signal about their expectations. They are saying to students, in effect, "Here is how I define excellence. Anyone here can produce work of such quality by applying sufficient effort." This is a powerful message for students; it brings excellence within their reach.

- *Greater student engagement.* When students are involved in performance tasks, particularly those that are highly authentic, they are more likely to be highly motivated in their work than if they are answering trivial types of questions. As a consequence of this engagement, the quality of student work is generally high.

Improved Communication with Families

Student work produced as part of a performance assessment is extremely meaningful to parents. If collected in a portfolio and used for parent conferences, these products can serve to document student learning (or its lack). If necessary, a student's work may be shown to families next to that of another (anonymous) student, to illustrate differences in performance. Such documentation may be very helpful to teachers in persuading a parent/guardian of the need for additional educational services.

If student work as part of performance assessment is maintained in a portfolio, however, the selections should be made with care. There are many possible uses of a portfolio, and students can benefit from the reflection that accompanies their own selection of "best work" entries. But as a documentation of student progress, items should be chosen that reflect student performance in all the important instructional goals. For example, if a math program consists of 5 strands taught through 12 units, the selections made should document each of the units, and all of the strands. These issues will be discussed more fully in Chapter 3.

☑ Professional Development Tip

Analyzing Types of Assessments

A discussion of the advantages and disadvantages of both traditional and non-traditional assessments can help teachers create or choose the kind of assessments that will elicit the evidence they need to make sound instructional decisions. Having teachers create a few selected-response items and a few performance assessment items targeting a skills-based standard, such as solving a linear equation, and a cognitively based standard, such as distinguishing between situations that can be modeled with linear functions and with exponential functions, will enhance their understanding of assessment. Individually scoring prepared responses to those items as they see fit and then comparing scores is likely to be quite interesting as the scores will probably be quite different. This can then lead the way to understanding the need for a commonly agreed upon rubric when scoring performance assessments, which will be discussed further in Chapter 6.

A Word about Grading

Many educators ask about converting the results of performance assessment to traditional grades. There are no easy answers to this question for the simple reason that the issue of grading does not lend itself to simplistic approaches. The reasons for this difficulty, however, are not related to performance assessment, but to the varied methods and purposes for assigning grades.

A "score" on a performance assessment is a straightforward matter; student work is evaluated against a clear standard and a judgment made as to where it stands against that standard. If students' grades are also intended (solely) to reflect the degree of mastery of the curriculum, then the score on the performance assessment can be translated in a fairly linear way to a grade. A score of "4" could be an "A," a "3" could be a "B," and so forth.

However, there are several reasons why such a procedure may not be ideal. For one thing, most teachers use other methods in addition to performance tasks to assess student learning. The typical evaluation plan used by a teacher will include traditional tests as well as performance items. Therefore, the results from different methods must be combined in some manner, including weighting some items more than others.

In addition, many teachers incorporate other elements in addition to achievement against a standard into a grade. They may want to build in the degree of progress from earlier work, for example, or the amount of effort or discipline displayed by a student. Alternatively, teachers may have offered some students a lot of coaching in their performance assessments (thereby using them also as teaching tools) and they may recognize that the students' performance reflects more than what they could do on their own.

Therefore, while performance assessments may not translate directly into grades, it may be a good idea to establish some connection between them, making the necessary provision for combining scores on different assessments. If this is done, it sends powerful messages to students. Primarily, such a procedure takes the mystery out of grading, and allows students to know in advance the criteria by which their work will be evaluated. In addition, it also conveys to students that high grades are within the reach of all students. Over time they recognize that if they work hard, they (all of them) can do well. In this situation, good grades are not rationed; all students whose work is at the highest standard can get an "A." As students come to internalize this awareness, and act upon it, it can transform a classroom into a far more purposeful place, and one in which students are concerned with the quality of their work.

Chapter Summary

◆ Traditional forms of assessment carry many disadvantages, which, when such tests are used exclusively, undermine the best intentions of teachers. These tests can evaluate only a narrow band of student learning and, even within that band, are extremely difficult to construct well.

◆ The use of performance assessment contributes many important benefits, beyond strictly measurement issues, to the culture of a classroom. These advantages are derived from clarity of criteria and standards, and benefit teachers, students, and parents.

3

Making an Evaluation Plan

Designing and implementing performance assessment entails a major investment of time and energy. To ensure that this investment is a wise one and that it yields the desired benefits, it is essential to work from a plan. How to develop such a plan and integrate it into a school or district's curriculum is the subject of this chapter.

A Curriculum Map

A useful approach to developing an assessment plan for mathematics instruction is to begin with a consideration of goals in the mathematics curriculum as a whole. An assessment plan, after all, should have as its goal the assessment of student learning in the curriculum; it makes no sense in isolation from the curriculum. Therefore, a plan for assessment should be created with the end in mind.

Critical Areas of Focus, Domains, and Clusters

A good place to start thinking about the assessment demands of the Common Core and other rigorous state standards is to consider the domains/strands and major clusters. Critical areas are identified by grade level, to provide a focus, to prioritize what's worth teaching and re-teaching for mastery, and what is supporting the work of the next grade.

These standards have had an enormous influence on the teaching of mathematics, and have caused educators everywhere to think more deeply about what they teach and how to engage their students in both conceptual understanding and procedural fluency with dual intensity.

For example, sixth-grade students complete their understanding of division of fractions and extend the notion of number to the system of rational numbers. In grade seven, students apply and extend prior understanding of operations with fractions to add, subtract, multiply, and divide rational numbers. Then in grade eight, they learn of numbers that are not rational but use rational numbers to approximate them. These content standards define grade-level proficiency and mastery, with a focus on fewer concepts understood more deeply. This results in teachers teaching less content at a higher level of cognitive demand. Students build on the foundations set in elementary grades to increase their understanding of numbers to the real number system by the end of middle school. This sets a solid foundation for working with real numbers as part of the complex number system in high school mathematics.

The eight Standards for Mathematical Practice describe the characteristics and traits of mathematically proficient students. These practices rest on important processes and proficiencies, much like the National Council of Teachers of Mathematics' (NCTM) process standards of problem solving, reasoning and proof, communication, representation and connections. They also reflect the proficiencies specified in the National Research Council's report *Adding It Up*: adaptive reasoning, strategic competence, conceptual understanding (comprehension of mathematical concepts, operations, and relations), procedural fluency (skill in carrying out procedures flexibly, accurately, efficiently, and appropriately), and productive disposition (habitual inclination to see mathematics as sensible, useful, and worthwhile, coupled with a belief in diligence and one's own efficacy).

School leaders and teachers that recognize how fundamental the practices are to learning the new content standards will certainly be interested in using performance assessments. Weaving the content standards with the practices has the potential to transform mathematical teaching and learning from what many experienced as students. Math content knowledge, the "what," must be addressed alongside of the "how" to support the belief that all students can—and must—develop proficiency with the mathematical practices.

School mathematics has traditionally been taught as a fixed set of facts and procedures for computing numerical and symbolic expressions to find one correct answer. Current practices are based on the beliefs that students should understand and reason with mathematical concepts, solve problems in diverse contexts, and develop a confidence in their own mathematical ability.

Active environments, where academic concepts are taught in a context of real-life problems, are more beneficial to students. These considerations—namely the shift in content to fewer topics studied in greater depth, close attention to the Standards for Mathematical Practice, and a clear progression of learning from grade to grade—have impacted and will continue to impact the design of teachers' curriculum maps.

Topics or Units

Most mathematics textbooks are still organized in a series of chapters or units, rather than clusters and standards. For example, in a typical middle school mathematics text, the chapters might be:

- Whole Numbers and Number Sense
- Integers
- Algebraic Expressions
- Equations and Lines
- Fractions
- Decimals
- Ratios, Proportions, and Percent
- Units of Measure and Geometry
- Statistics and Probability

Clearly, some of the topics fit well with some of the standards. For example, the concepts taught in the "Units of Measure and Geometry" chapter address the goals in the "geometry" domain. But some of the other connections are not nearly so obvious. In which chapter, for instance, is material related to "mathematics as communication" or "modeling" found? If educators are committed to addressing all the goals stated or implied in the CCSSM Standards, or the equivalent document from their own state or district, then they must match the topics or units they teach with the goals inherent in those standards.

The best technique to use for this purpose is a matrix, such as is described in the next section, and a sample of which is presented in Table 3.1. This table focuses on the content standards for unit planning; however, teachers and curriculum planners should also keep the eight Standards for Mathematical Practice in mind as they create lessons.

Creating the Curriculum Map

Across the top of the matrix are listed the domains of the grade level. Down the left-hand side are listed all the topics or units in the year's curriculum,

22 ◆ Making an Evaluation Plan

Table 3.1 Curriculum/Assessment Planning Matrix

Unit	Ratios and Proportional Relationships	The Number System	Expressions and Equations	Geometry	Statistics and Probability	Functions

organized, insofar as can be known, in sequence. Then, for each unit or topic, teachers should consider which of the standards the topic addresses, and place a check mark in the corresponding box.

What results from this process is a map of the curriculum, demonstrating the ways in which the different domains, clusters and standards are (or can be, given the textbook in use) addressed in each of the topics of the curriculum.

The map may reveal large gaps in the curriculum. If, for example, the curriculum map shows that some of the standards are not adequately addressed by the program in use, then some adjustments must be made to include supplements. It is also possible that the curriculum has content that is no longer relevant to that grade level. For example, probability. In which case, that content can be omitted in favor of the major work of the grade.

In some cases, the content might be aligned, but the Mathematical Practices are not developed in the lessons. For example, "reasoning and explaining" may be done exclusively by the teacher, and not an expectation for student behavior. In that case, educators have to determine in which topics they could develop that skill, and how. Once determined, they can then add check marks to the appropriate boxes. For instance, teachers could decide to add to each of their units a goal for modeling mathematics and using tools precisely, and identify the specific manipulatives and visual models they will use in the context of the lessons. In that way, they would adequately address all the content and process standards.

Assessment Methodologies

Once the curriculum map has been produced, educators (teachers or curriculum specialists) must determine how each of the content and process standards, and each of the clusters, are to be assessed. Some will lend themselves to traditional testing; others will require more complex performance assessment.

The Role of Traditional Testing

Some mathematics curriculum goals may be assessed through traditional testing. It is, and will always be, important for students to be able to perform accurate computations, to use technology to show they can identify attributes of geometric shapes and apply formulas. For all these reasons, educators would be ill-advised to abandon the use of traditional tests as part of their total assessment plan.

However, traditional testing is limited in what it can achieve. As teachers survey the curriculum map they have produced, they discover that some of the check marks they have written simply do not lend themselves to a multiple-choice or short-answer test. What kind of test, for example, could one construct that would assess students on the communication of ideas? Or on the use of models and tools?

Moreover, many educators argue that the use of traditional tests, even in those areas of the curriculum where they seem to be best suited, can do actual harm because some students, and their teachers, confuse procedural knowledge with conceptual understanding. That is, students learn a procedure, an algorithm, for getting "the right answer" with little or no understanding of how or why the procedure works, of where it would be useful, or of what the algorithm accomplishes. Therefore, they can take a test and solve problems correctly, but with poor conceptual understanding. And if the assessment procedures used do not reveal that lack of understanding, the students may move along to more complex concepts, ones that build on the previous ones, with an increasingly shaky foundation.

Thus, while traditional tests may be highly useful in assessing certain aspects of the mathematics curriculum, they should be used with caution and with full awareness of their limitations.

The Place for Performance Assessment

Performance assessment is the technique of choice for evaluating student understanding of much of the mathematics curriculum. When students are asked to complete a task—when they are asked to explain their thinking— they reveal their understanding of complex topics.

Sometimes performance assessment in mathematics can consist of a small addition to traditional testing. For example, students might be asked to solve a fairly traditional problem, but then asked to explain why they selected the approach they did. Their explanation reveals their understanding of the process, or their lack of it, and serves to assess their skill in the communication of mathematical ideas.

In addition, the authentic application of mathematical procedures is highly motivational to students. Many students regard the applications problems (word problems) that they encounter in most mathematics textbooks with disbelief; their reaction is frequently one of "who cares?" With some thought, however, most teachers can create situations that students in their classes might actually encounter, which require the application of the mathematical ideas included in a given unit. The creation and adaption of such a task is the subject of Chapter 5.

A Plan to Get Started

The idea of creating (or even adapting) performance tasks for all those areas of the mathematics curriculum for which they would be well suited can be daunting. After all, if students as well as teachers are unfamiliar with such an approach, it is likely to take more time than planned. And because it is unfamiliar, everyone involved is likely to encounter unexpected difficulties. How, then, should one begin?

Not all standards are created equal, as indicated in Dr. Norman Webb's Depth of Knowledge (DOK). Dr. Webb identified four levels for assessing the DOK of content standards and assessment items, as stated below.

◆ *Level 1 (Recall)* includes the recall of information such as a fact, definition, term, or a simple procedure, as well as performing a simple algorithm or applying a formula. Key words that signify a Level 1 include "identify," "recall," "recognize," "use," and "measure."

◆ *Level 2 (Skill/Concept)* includes the engagement of some mental processing beyond a habitual response. A Level 2 assessment item requires students to make some decisions as to how to approach the problem. Keywords that generally distinguish a Level 2 include "classify," "organize," "estimate," "make observations," "collect and display data," and "compare data." These actions imply more than one step.

◆ *Level 3 (Strategic Thinking)* requires reasoning, planning, using evidence, and a higher level of thinking than the previous two levels. In most instances, requiring students to explain their thinking and make conjectures. The cognitive demands at Level 3 are complex and abstract. Level 3 activities include drawing conclusions from observations; citing evidence and developing a logical argument for concepts; and using concepts to solve problems.

◆ *Level 4 (Extended Thinking)* requires complex reasoning, planning, developing, and thinking most likely over an extended period of time. At Level 4, students should be required to make several connections—relate ideas *within* the content area or *among* content areas. Level 4 activities include designing and conducting experiments; making connections between a finding and related concepts and phenomena; combining and synthesizing ideas into new concepts; and critiquing experimental designs.

Traditional assessments can measure Level 1 and 2 standards with multiple-choice and short-response items, but performance tasks are often better suited to assess standards written at a Level 2 and beyond. Examining the verbs in the standards will provide teachers with important information on how cognitively demanding the assessment task needs to be.

In general, one should start small. Once the techniques and practices of performance assessment are well understood, and once teachers and students both have some experience in the methodology, performance tasks may be used frequently, particularly if they are small ones. However, when beginning, it is recommended that teachers use performance tasks infrequently, at a rate, for example, of four to six per year. Such a schedule permits teachers the time to create or adapt their tasks to ensure that they accomplish their desired purposes and to evaluate student work carefully. If only one or two tasks are administered per quarter, they should be those that are likely to reveal the most information about student understanding.

Once teachers have acquired experience in the use of performance tasks, they may want to use them more frequently and more informally. However, even with experience, few teachers will administer more than two or three such tasks per month.

Chapter Summary

◆ A curriculum map can be used to define which units or topics in a curriculum may be used to help students acquire the knowledge and skills inherent in a state's mathematics curriculum. The map is created by local educators, using their own textbook, exercising professional judgment, to ensure that all the standards are being met comprehensively.

◆ Based on the curriculum map, educators can create an evaluation plan. This plan should include both traditional testing and performance assessment. As they move to performance assessment, teachers are advised to start small, with tasks that are written at a higher DOK level.

4

Understanding Quality Performance Tasks

Quality performance tasks are not simply something fun to do with one's students; they are not merely activities. While they may involve student activity, and they may be fun, they are highly purposeful. Performance tasks are designed to assess learning, and that fundamental purpose must remain foremost in the mind of anyone using them. The criteria for quality presented in this chapter will be essential as you consider adaptation and creation of performance tasks. These criteria center around three important interrelated questions:

- ◆ Does the task assess the content I want to assess?
- ◆ Does it meaningfully engage students?
- ◆ Does it provide a fair measurement of students' understanding?

The criteria that follow paint a picture of a quality performance task. A rubric that explicates each criterion and distinguishes between a quality performance task and one in need of improvement is included at the end of the chapter in Table 4.1.

Purpose

Any discussion of quality as it relates to performance tasks must necessarily begin with a clear understanding of assessment and the specific goals associated with performance assessment. In Chapter 2, we outline several benefits of performance assessment, including clarity as to criteria and standards, professional dialogue about criteria and standards, improved student work, high expectations, and student engagement.

A good performance task must assess what we want it to assess. It must, in other words, be aligned to the instructional goals we are interested in. Furthermore, the task should be designed in such a way that a student can complete the task correctly only by using the knowledge and skills being assessed.

We should never underestimate our students in this regard. While most students are not devious, most try to complete a task with as little risk and/ or effort as possible. If they see an easy way to do the task, even by short-circuiting our intentions, they may well do it that way. Teachers should attempt, therefore, to create tasks that are as tight as possible, without being unduly rigid.

Additionally, while content standards have traditionally been front and center when developing assessment materials, standards-based reforms have provided us with a host of competencies, practices, and proficiencies that students should demonstrate as they engage in the kinds of open-ended problems that comprise performance tasks. Including an assessment of these practices takes advantage of the very nature of performance tasks. Excluding them from the assessment process would squander an opportunity to gather great evidence of student understanding.

☑ **Professional Development Tip**

Working with Colleagues to Align Content and Tasks

Engaging with colleagues is one way to deepen our understanding of the degree to which the task is tightly aligned to the identified content, often a standard or group of standards. In a collaborative teacher team meeting, begin by having all participants work out the task. Doing this has several benefits, including illustrating a variety of solution pathways. The opportunity to work with teachers from different grades can prove a valuable opportunity to collect a range of diverse responses to the task. You may wish to ask colleagues to respond to the task as if they were a student. Once the responses are generated, take time to closely analyze them. You may wish to refer to your state or district standards to identify the degree to which the responses to the task meet the demands of those standards. In doing so, you can better answer the question, "Does the task assess the content I want to assess?"

Engaging

Another critical feature of performance tasks is that they are engaging to students; it is essential that they be of interest and that students want to put forth their best effort. This suggests that the questions asked have intrinsic merit so that students don't read the question and respond, "So what?" or, "Who cares?" Engagement, as used here, refers to more than mere compliance, more than a student following a set of directions provided by the teacher. Here, we mean that quality performance tasks provide opportunities for students to think deeply and critically, to reason and construct mathematical arguments, and to make sense of problems that aren't merely an application of an algorithmic process already learned—and *ideally* to get students to want to do these things.

Engaging students in meaningful and purposeful work is one of the teacher's greatest challenges. But it's also a key goal to improving instruction and, ultimately, student achievement in mathematics. If we hold as a goal the preparation of students for an increasingly technological society that demands quantitative reasoning in both daily life and the world of work, we must commit to *engage* students in mathematics. Doing so also fosters students' engagement in a set of practices—variously referred to as habits of mind, mathematical processes, or mathematical practices—that have been at the center of mathematics reform for the better part of the past two decades.

Students are engaged when they study interesting or provocative questions. Often, these questions require students to construct arguments which, by their very nature, require rigorous mathematical thinking. For example, a task might require students to answer questions such as, "When subtracting, what happens to the minuend when the subtrahend decreases by 5? What happens when it increases by 5?" Elementary school students could answer these questions empirically by working through several examples. But it could also be proved algebraically and represented symbolically in middle school grades. In either case, these questions are puzzles, and puzzles are games, which generate student interest.

How does one find or create engaging tasks? As with so much else in education, professional judgment is the key. Successful instructional activities can be a good place to begin; most teachers know which activities, or which types of activities, are successful with their students. One of these activities, when adapted to the demands of assessment, might make a good performance task. And when reviewing tasks that others have created, one important criterion to always bear in mind is whether the task is likely to be engaging to students.

Authentic

Related to engagement is the issue of authenticity. Students tend to be more interested in those situations that resemble "real life" rather than those which are completely divorced from any practical application. This means that the task asks students to solve a realistic problem with clear and immediate applications in the real world. For instance, a task might require students to use transformations to animate a shape on the coordinate plane as part of their study of geometry.

In addition, performance tasks that reflect the "messiness" of real life make demands on students that more sanitized situations do not. For example, real-life situations require that students make assumptions and identify constraints. Students might solve a system of linear equations in mathematics. Or, in a more authentic task, they might be asked to identify whether two different cell phone plans cost the same amount of money. Making a recommendation about the cheaper plan would require that students make assumptions about usage patterns. This is more like the decision an adult makes in the face of a cell phone marketplace that consists of many providers, different levels of call quality, and different pricing models. It is preferable to design or adapt performance tasks that represent authentic applications of knowledge and skill. This has the advantage of requiring students to use their knowledge and skill in much the same way it is used by adult practitioners in that field. A template to be used for designing authentic tasks is provided in Figure 4.1 at the end of the chapter.

However, much of mathematics is highly formal and abstract and authenticity is not always possible. While teachers care that students can apply their mathematical knowledge to practical situations, there is much of mathematics, such as properties of real numbers, which is internal to the discipline. But such knowledge must be assessed, and a constructed-response question is preferable to a multiple-choice item. However, such a question will probably not reflect authentic application.

Enables Assessment of Individuals

Many performance tasks that sound imaginative are designed to be completed by students working in groups. And while such tasks may be valuable instructional activities and are certainly fun for the students, they cannot be used for the assessment of individuals. Assessment, after all, concerns the evaluation of individual learning; a performance task in which the contributions of different individuals are obscured cannot be used for such evaluation.

It is possible, of course, to design a performance task that includes both group and individual elements. For example, a group of students may be given some data and asked to analyze it. However, if the analysis is done as a group, each student should be required to produce an independent summary of what the data shows, and each individual's paper should be evaluated independently.

However, even in such a situation, the information for the teacher is somewhat compromised. When reading the work of an individual, a teacher knows only what that student could produce after having participated in a group with other students. With a different group of peers, that same student might have demonstrated much greater, or far less, understanding.

In general, then, it is preferable to create individual performance tasks if these are to be used solely for assessment purposes. If the goal also includes instructional purposes, then compromises on the individuality of the assessment tasks may be necessary.

Contains Clear Directions for Students

Any good performance task includes directions for students that are both complete and unambiguous. This is a fundamental principle of equity and good measurement. Students should never be in doubt about what it is they are to do on a performance task; the directions should be clear and complete. This does not preclude a task that includes the "messiness" described earlier, messiness that might require students to make assumptions when faced with incomplete data, for example. And it does not mean that the directions should be lengthy; on the contrary, shorter directions are preferable to longer ones.

Second, the directions should specifically ask students to do everything on which they will be evaluated. For example, if one of the assessment criteria for a mathematics problem involves the organization of information, students should be specifically instructed to "present their information in an organized manner," or some such wording.

Related to the question of directions is that of scaffolding, that is, how much support should students receive in accomplishing the performance task? For example, in a mathematics problem that involves a multi-step solution, should the students be prompted for each step, or is that part of the problem? The answer to this question relates to the purposes of the

Table 4.1 Performance Task Analytic Rubric

Element	In Need of Revision (Limited) (1)	Acceptable Task (2)	High Quality Task (3)
Engaging	◆ May be a problem similar to one already studied or of limited interest to students	◆ Some thought and persistence required to complete the task, though some aspects may only require application of previously learned procedures	◆ Provide students with a worthy question that requires thought and persistence to solve ◆ Task requires reasoning
Authentic	◆ Reflects a situation that wouldn't be encountered in the real world	◆ May reflect a situation that is similar to the real world, with parameters that make it somewhat artificial	◆ Reflects, to the degree possible, a real world application of the content targeted in the assessment
Clear	◆ Directions are unclear ◆ Evaluation criteria are not shared with students in advance of performance, either through a rubric or directions that specify the components of a satisfactory performance	◆ Directions are clear, but may not be sufficiently concise ◆ Evaluation criteria are partially shared with students, most likely through some direction regarding satisfactory performance or some rubric elements shared with students. May contain vague statements regarding evaluation, e.g., "students will be evaluated on presentation and clarity of work shown"	◆ Directions are clear and concise ◆ Evaluation criteria are shared clearly and precisely with students, e.g., through a rubric or directions which specify the components of a satisfactory performance
Elicits Desired Knowledge and Skill	◆ Task doesn't require that students have desired knowledge for successful completion	◆ Partially aligned to desired knowledge and skill, or may require other knowledge and skills (not a prerequisite of the desired knowledge and skills) to be successfully completed ◆ Includes opportunities in which students could demonstrate practices/"habits of mind," but doesn't require them to demonstrate satisfactory performance	◆ Aligned to relevant standards and curriculum ◆ Assesses mathematical content as well as practices/"habits of mind" ◆ Limits students' ability to demonstrate understandings other than those targeted with a correct and complete solution
Enables Assessment of Individuals	◆ The product is a result of group work in which one group member's contributions are indistinguishable from the contributions of other group members	◆ The product is a result of some group but also includes some work that is independently completed	◆ The task requires significant independent work, submitted independently of group work

Figure 4.1 Performance Task: Authentic Simulation

Outcome: _____

Topic: _____

You are (student or adult role or profession)

Who has been asked by (audience or superior)

To (accomplish a specific task)

Using (resources)

Under the constraints of (as found in such a situation)

Your work will be judged according to (criteria)

(Attach a rubric)

Source: Based on worksheets from the High Success Network and CLASS.

assessment, and the age and skill level of the students. Less scaffolding is more authentic than more scaffolding; most problems are not presented to us with an outline of how to solve them. In general it is preferable to provide students with problems, with no scaffolding, that represent the optimal challenge for them to determine the proper approach on their own. An intermediate position is to present the problem, with no scaffolding, and then offer "tips" to the student to consider as needed. These tips can contain suggestions that, if followed, would provide guidance as to a possible approach to the problem.

Chapter Summary

◆ Good performance tasks share a number of important criteria. They elicit the desired knowledge and skill, meaningfully engage students, and fairly measure students' learning. These should be considered as tasks are designed and adapted.

◆ Engaging tasks are more than merely "interesting." They require reasoning and student engagement with a set of habits of mind/mathematical practices that reflect what successful mathematicians do.

5

Creating and Adapting
Performance Tasks

The evaluation plan that results from the analysis of curriculum outcomes and topics (determined in Chapter 3) provides the guidelines needed to actually design performance tasks. As part of that plan, educators will have decided which standards have a higher cognitive demand and Depth of Knowledge (DOK), or choose a cluster of standards that reflect the major work of the grade. Often standards that begin with the word "understand" are a good fit for a performance task.

In the design of performance tasks, a number of factors must be taken into consideration to achieve these ends. These are described in this chapter.

Size of Performance Tasks

Performance tasks may be large or small. Unique among assessment types, large tasks often take on many of the characteristics of instructional units in that students learn from engaging in the task. Large tasks, commonly referred to as projects, may require a week or more to complete. They are typically complex and authentic, and require students to synthesize information from many sources. For example, a large task might require students to synthesize their understanding of geometry and probability to determine the likelihood that a parachute landing will be in an open area of a town. This task requires that students work flexibly with a set of constraints, e.g., the area of the town, the area occupied by the buildings, and the relationship between the open area and the entire area of the town. Small tasks, on the other hand, are more like open-ended questions in which students solve a problem and explain their reasoning. These may be completed in a single class period or less. Naturally, there are a range of performance tasks that may be of medium length and complexity.

In deciding whether to use performance tasks that are large or small, educators must take a number of factors into account. These are outlined below.

Purpose

Teachers should be very clear about their purpose in using the performance task. What do they hope and plan to derive from it? Are their purposes purely those of assessment, or do they hope to accomplish some instructional purposes as well?

- *Small tasks are primarily suitable for purely assessment purposes.* If a teacher has taught a concept, for example, the distinction and relationship between area and volume, and simply wants to know that students have understood that concept, then a small performance task is desirable. Such a task will ask students to solve a relatively small problem, to explain their thinking, and to show their work. However, it will not, in itself, also contain activities to be completed as part of the task. The task itself is designed primarily for assessment.

- *Large tasks carry instructional purposes as well as assessment ones.* Occasionally, a teacher will want students to truly learn new content as a result of completing an assessment task. If so, a larger task, spread over a number of days, involving many sub-activities, will accomplish this purpose better than a small task.

- *Culminating assessments require the assessments of a broader range of skills and conceptual understanding.* Large performance tasks are particularly well suited to culminating assessments because they tap a number of different types of skills and understandings. Smaller performance tasks can be combined to assess a larger instructional unit as a culminating assessment. However, if performance tasks are for the purpose of assessing a small part of the curriculum, small tasks are more useful since they can be administered frequently and the results used for adjusting instruction. The purpose of the assessment will be a major factor, then, in determining whether performance tasks should be large or small.

Curriculum Pressure and Time Demands

Generally speaking, when teachers are under pressure to "cover" many topics in the curriculum, and consequently have little time to spend on any one topic, they may find that small performance tasks are all that they have time for. Large tasks, while they include many benefits not derived from small ones, do require substantial amounts of time, frequently more than many teachers can devote to them. Indeed, small performance tasks are a great (and manageable) way for teachers to begin the use of performance assessment in their classrooms for a number of reasons:

◆ they are easier to construct or adapt from third party sources;
◆ they are easily administered in a short amount of time;
◆ they broaden the kinds of understandings that can be assessed.

Skill in Getting Started

Most educators, when they are just beginning to use performance tasks, are unsure of what they are doing; in such situations it is a good idea to use the "start small" principle. For example, when not sure whether the directions to students on a task are clear, it is better to discover that after the students have spent a class period, rather than a week, completing the task. Less time has been devoted to it and there may well be an opportunity to attempt another version of the same task, or a different task, later.

The Design Process

Now that your purpose for creating a performance task is clearly in mind, it is time to create one. What process should be followed? While there are several possible approaches, an effective one is described below.

Begin with a Clear Goal in Mind

As mentioned earlier in this chapter, a critical feature of a well-designed performance task is a clear alignment to the instructional goal(s) in which teachers are interested. In many cases, performance tasks will be designed to assess the major goals of an instructional unit. In that case, it is worth beginning by reviewing the standards and learning goals the author (whether a group of teachers or a curriculum publisher) of the instructional unit has identified. The size of the performance task and the instructional unit must be considered when determining "how much" the task will assess.

It is problematic for a performance task to focus too narrowly on a skill or too broadly on too many concepts. With the development of the Common Core State Standards for Mathematics, it is important to attend to goals that reflect both the standards for mathematical content as well as the Standards for Mathematical Practice. In fact, performance tasks are uniquely positioned to provide teachers with assessments of students' mastery of the mathematical practices.

Create an Initial Design

With the specifications and criteria in mind, create an initial draft of a performance task to assess a given combination of student understanding and skill. This task may be created using the format provided in Figure 5.1 at the end of the chapter, and it may, if authenticity is desired, follow the template offered in Figure 4.1. This initial draft should be considered as just that, an initial draft—it will almost certainly be revised later in the process. A good way to begin the design process is to preview the vast number of performance tasks available online, in commercial programs, and in professional texts, such as this one, to get a sense of the style and type of task you'd like to develop. This is a critical step and should not be overlooked.

☑ **Professional Development Tip**

Designing Prototype Tasks

As a first step in designing performance tasks, consider gathering teachers at the same grade-level or who teach the same subject or course. Identify a set of standards, including both content standards and mathematical proficiencies/habits of mind, or a unit of study from your curriculum, and have each teacher generate a seed idea or prototype for a performance task designed to assess that content. Have each teacher type their prototype task or seed idea and place on posters in the room where the team meeting will take place.

Once the group is assembled, members should conduct a carousel walk, where appropriate solving a prototype task or analyzing a seed idea. After cycling through all proposals, group members return to the poster at which they started and provide two pieces of feedback and one piece of advice, as follows:

(continued)

> *(continued)*
>
> ◆ Identify a strength of the performance task prototype or idea and write on a sticky note to share. For example, you might notice that the task is well aligned to the content standards identified in the unit of study.
>
> ◆ Identify an area of growth or next step and share on a sticky note. For example, you might notice that the task could be solved using repeated addition, even though the unit is focused on the multiplicative relationship in equivalent ratios.
>
> ◆ Last, share a recommendation on how to improve the task. For example, you might suggest that the task include directions to students to show their work to enable better assessment of conceptual understanding.
>
> At the end of this exercise, your team will have several possible seed ideas that can be adapted, developed, merged or discarded. In any case, you'll have harnessed the power of collective thinking to begin the process of drafting a performance task.

Obtain Colleague Review

If possible, persuade one or more colleagues to review your work. These may be teachers who work in the same discipline as you or with the same age students, or they may be teachers with very different responsibilities. Both approaches have their advantages and their drawbacks.

Teachers with different responsibilities are more likely to catch ambiguity or lack of clarity in the directions to students than are teachers who are as expert in the field as you are. On the other hand, expert colleagues are better able to provide feedback on the content being addressed in the task and spot situations in which it is not completely valid; that is, situations in which students would be able to complete the task successfully without the desired knowledge and skill. Therefore, a colleague review that includes a combination of content experts and non-experts is ideal.

Pilot Task with Students

Not until a performance task is tried with students is it possible to know whether it can accomplish its desired purpose. Only then can teachers know whether the directions are clear, whether all elements are properly requested, and whether the task truly elicits the desired knowledge and skill.

Figure 5.1 Performance Task Design Worksheet

Task title: _____

Course _____

Unit or topic _____

Standard(s) addressed:

Brief description of the task (what students must do, and what product will result): *(For short performance tasks, include problem here.)*

Directions to the students:

Criteria to be used to evaluate student responses:

40 ◆ Creating and Adapting Performance Tasks

Careful attention should be paid to the verbs in the standards themselves, to determine whether the child is able to demonstrate a complete or fragile understanding of the concepts.

Piloting with students is also the only way to know the degree to which the task is engaging and accessible to them. Students are likely to be honest in their reaction to a performance task perhaps more honest than their teachers would like. While it is possible to collect their feedback formally, it is generally evident from their level of engagement and from the quality of their responses whether the task is a good one or not, or how it could be improved.

Revise Performance Task

As a result of the colleague review and the pilot with students, the draft task will, no doubt, require some revision. This revision might be a major rewrite or it might be a minor "tweak" in order to make the task clearer, less cumbersome, or differently slanted.

Once revised, the task is ready for the formal process of rubric design discussed in Chapter 7. However, teachers should be aware that the task may need further revision after the scoring rubric is written—that exercise frequently reveals inadequacies (usually minor) in the task itself.

Adapting Existing Performance Tasks

Often, you can save time and effort by adapting an existing task for your own use. Many state departments of education have created prototype tasks, and textbook publishers often offer tasks as part of their package.

Matching Outcomes, Topics, and Students

The first step in identifying tasks suitable for adaptation is to match the outcomes and topics assessed by the task with those in one's own curriculum. The performance tasks in this book have been aligned with the Common Core State Standards. By examining those alignments, educators can determine whether a given task would be of value to them in assessing student mastery of their own curriculum.

It is unlikely that such a match will be perfect. Frequently, a performance task will ask students to perform an operation or complete an activity that students in a given class have not yet learned. Even tasks well aligned to the Common Core State Standards may not be well aligned to the scope and sequence of topics addressed in a particular curriculum or with a particular group of students. Alternatively, a scoring rubric will include criteria that do not reflect a district's curriculum or priorities. In those cases, either the task or the rubric will have to be adjusted.

Chapter Summary

◆ The size of a performance task is best determined by its purpose (immediate or culminating assessment, or instruction) and by the time constraints and experience of the teacher. In general, it is recommended that teachers begin their efforts with performance assessment using tasks which are small rather than large. This provides the opportunity to experiment with a new methodology in a way that carries low stakes for success, for both the students and the teacher.

◆ The process of task design has several steps, all of which should be completed. A performance task should not be used for actual assessment until it has been piloted with students. This suggests that at least a year will elapse between the decision to embark on a program of performance assessment and the implementation of such a system.

◆ In order to determine whether an existing performance task can be used as written, educators must match the task's outcomes and topics with those in their curriculum, and consider their own students.

6

Using Rubrics to Evaluate
Complex Performance

A Nonschool Example

All of the principles involved in the evaluation of complex performance
may be illustrated by an everyday example—going to a restaurant. Reading
through this example readers address, in a more familiar form, all of the
issues that they encounter in designing systems of performance assessment
for classroom use. Moreover, it becomes evident that the methods for
evaluating performance reflect, at their heart, only common sense.

The Situation

Imagine that we are opening a restaurant in your town and that we are now
ready to hire servers. We know that it is important that the servers be skilled,
so we want to hire the best that we can find. As part of our search, we have
decided to eat in some existing restaurants to see if there are people working
in these establishments that we can lure to our restaurant. Consequently, we
are preparing to embark on our search mission.

The Criteria

How will we know what to look for? We must determine the five or six most
important qualities we would watch for in a good server. But because our
focus is on "performance," we should list only those qualities that are visible
to a customer (such as appearance), and not other qualities which, while they

might be important to an employer (such as getting to work on time), are not seen by a customer.

A reasonable list of criteria includes such qualities as courtesy, appearance, responsiveness, knowledge, coordination, and accuracy. It is important to write the criteria using neutral rather than positive words. That is, for reasons that will become apparent shortly, we should write "appearance" rather than "neat."

These criteria could, of course, become a checklist. That is, we could eat in a restaurant and determine whether our server was courteous, or responsive, or knowledgeable, and so forth. We could answer each of the items with a "yes" or "no," and then count the "yeses." However, life tends to be more complex than a checklist—a server might be *somewhat* knowledgeable, *mostly* accurate, *a little bit* coordinated.

How do we accommodate these degrees of performance? How do we design a system that respects the complexity of the performance, yet that allows us to compare two or more individuals. The answer is to create a rubric, a scoring guide.

The Scoring Guide or Rubric
Table 6.1 is a rubric, which is simply a guide for evaluating performance.

Table 6.1 Server Evaluation Rubric

	Level One	Level Two	Level Three	Level Four
Courtesy				
Appearance				
Responsiveness				
Knowledge				
Coordination				
Accuracy				

The criteria that are important for servers in our fledgling restaurant are listed in the left column. Across the top, are columns for different levels of performance. In this case, there are four levels. The double-line between Levels Two and Three indicates that performance at Levels Three and Four is acceptable, but performance at Levels One and Two is unacceptable. We could, then, broadly define the different levels as:

Level One: unacceptable

Level Two: almost, but not quite, good enough

Level Three: acceptable

Level Four: exemplary

In each box, then, we would write descriptions of actual performance that would represent each level for each criterion. For example, for "coordination" we might decide that an individual at Level One is someone who actually spilled an entire bowl of soup, or a cup of coffee, or who could not handle a tray of dishes; an individual at Level Two is someone who spilled a little coffee in the saucer, or who spilled some water while filling the glasses; a person at Level Three is someone who spilled nothing; and a person at Level Four is someone who balanced many items without mishap.

We could fill in the entire chart with such descriptions, and we would then be ready to go evaluate prospective employees. A possible profile might look like Table 6.2:

Table 6.2 A Completed Server Rubric

Name: Jamie Jones   Restaurant: Hilltop Cafe

	Level One	Level Two	Level Three	Level Four
Courtesy		X		
Appearance				X
Responsiveness			X	
Knowledge	X			
Coordination				X
Accuracy			X	

We still have to decide, of course, whether to hire this individual, or whether this individual was preferable to another candidate whose scores were all "3s." That is, we still have to determine how to arrive at a composite score for each individual so that we can compare them.

If we were using this approach for supervision or coaching rather than for hiring, we would not need to combine scores on the different criteria. We could use the scores for feedback and coaching. For example, because this individual is, apparently, not very knowledgeable, we could provide assistance in that area. We could then work on courtesy, and make sure that customers feel comfortable around this person. That is, for supervision or coaching purposes, the system is diagnostic and enables us to provide specific and substantive feedback on areas needing improvement.

Measurement and Practical Issues

When we contemplate applying these principles to the evaluation of student performance, we encounter a number of issues which, while not technically complex, must be addressed before this approach can be implemented. It should be borne in mind that most teachers have rubrics in their minds for student performance; they apply these every time they grade a student's paper. However, communication is vastly improved if educators can be explicit about the criteria they use in evaluating student work and about what their expectations are. Achieving this clarity requires the teacher to address a number of technical and practical issues.

The Number and Type of Criteria

For a given performance, how many criteria should we have? For example, when evaluating a persuasive essay, how many different things should we look for? Should we evaluate organization separately from structure? What about the use of language or, specifically, the use of vocabulary; or correct spelling and mechanics? What about sentence structure and organization? Should we consider the essay's impact on us, the reader? Is it important that we be persuaded by the argument?

Clearly, some of these elements are related to one another: it would be difficult, in a persuasive essay, for example, to have good use of language independently of the vocabulary used. However, other criteria are completely separate from one another. A student's inadequacies in mechanics and spelling, for example, will not affect the persuasiveness of the argument, unless it is so poor as to hinder communication.

The number of criteria used should reflect, insofar as is possible, those aspects of performance that are simultaneously important and independent of one another. With primary students, three or four criteria that demonstrate organization and approach, mathematical accuracy, and oral or written presentations are appropriate. The criteria should reflect the age and skill of the students. With young children or students with special needs, for example, it might be necessary to identify specific aspects of punctuation that are evaluated—proper use of capital letters, commas, and semicolons—whereas for high school students these may all be clustered under "punctuation" and can include all aspects of mechanics.

However, when criteria are clustered in such a way that they include several elements, these should be specifically identified. Just as "appearance" in the server example might include the person's uniform, condition of the hair and nails, and general grooming, individual criteria should specify what elements are included. For example, "use of language" might include richness of vocabulary, use of persuasive words, and proper use of specialized terms.

Moreover, the criteria should reflect those aspects of performance that are truly most important, not merely those that are easiest to see or count. Thus, a rubric for writing should include more than spelling and mechanics; a rubric for problem solving should include criteria dealing with the student's thought processes, the use of models and strategies.

A rubric should not include so many criteria that it is difficult to use. On the other hand, it should include every element considered important. As a general rule, because most people cannot hold more than five or six items in their mind simultaneously, rubrics should not contain more than five or six criteria.

Analytic vs. Holistic Rubrics

The server rubric developed in the previous section is an example of an *analytic* rubric, that is, different criteria are identified and levels of performance are described for each. A similar rubric, but with different criteria defined and described, is usable in the classroom to *analyze* the strengths and weaknesses of student work.

With a *holistic* rubric, on the other hand, the features of performance on all criteria for a given score are combined so that it is possible, for example, to describe a "Level Two" or a "Level Four" server. Such holistic judgments are necessary when a single score, such as on an advanced placement test, must be given. However, compromises are necessary, because an individual piece of work usually does not include all the features of a certain level. Therefore, analytic rubrics are recommended for classroom use, because they provide much more complete information for feedback to students.

How Many Points on the Scale?

In the server example, we identified four points on the scale. That was an arbitrary decision; we could have selected more or less. Performance on any criterion, after all, falls along a continuum; designating points on a scale represents, to some degree, a compromise between practical demands and the complexity of real performance. However, in deciding on the number of points to use, there are several important considerations to remember:

- *Fineness of distinctions.* More points offer the opportunity to make very fine distinctions between levels of performance. However, scales with many points are time-consuming to use because the differences between the points are likely to be small.
- *Even vs. odd.* In general, an even number of points is preferable to an odd number. This relates to the measurement principle of central tendency, which states that many people, if given the opportunity, will assign a score in the middle of a range. If there is no middle, as on a scale with an even number of points, they are required to make a commitment to one side or the other.

However, these considerations apply to rubrics that are constructed for application to a single activity or type of performance. For *developmental* rubrics, a large number of points may be preferable. In a developmental rubric, students' performance over an extended period of time with respect to important concepts and skills is monitored on a single rubric. Such rubrics are representative of learning progressions in which understanding ranges from a rudimentary level to an advanced level in a single domain. For example, the proportional reasoning learning progression developed by Baxter and Junker (Baxter & Junker as cited in R. Weaver & B. Junker, *Model Specification on Cognitive Assessment of Proportional Reasoning,* 2004, http://lib.stat.cmu.edu/~brian/bjtrs.html) ranges from an intuitive understanding of at which students can answer questions about fairness to a level at which students have a generalized model for solving proportionality problems and a repertoire of solution strategies. A student in early elementary school may have an intuitive understanding of proportional reasoning but may not have a generalized model for solving problems involving proportionality until they are in middle or high school. A developmental rubric with many points on the scale is extremely useful in proportional reasoning and in other domains because it can be used to chart a student's progress with respect to important concepts and skills over an extended period of time providing an informed direction for instruction that moves students to the next level in a learning progression.

Dividing Line between Acceptable and Unacceptable Performance

It is important to decide, at the outset, where the line will be between acceptable and unacceptable performance. A dichotomous sort (good enough/not good enough) forces teachers to determine what work is proficient. This activity is at the heart of setting a standard because teachers thereby communicate, to their colleagues as well as to their students, the quality of work they expect.

In the server example, the line between acceptable and unacceptable performance was established between Levels Two and Three. This, too, is arbitrary; it could just as well been put between Levels One and Two. When determining where to place the dividing line, educators should consider several points:

- ◆ *Use.* If a scoring rubric is to be used for formative evaluation, it is helpful to identify several levels of unacceptable performance so that teachers can know quickly whether a student's performance on a certain criterion is close to being acceptable, or is far away. Such knowledge can guide further instruction. On the other hand, if a rubric is to be used to make a summative judgment only, then it is less important whether a student's performance is close to the cut-off point; unacceptable is unacceptable, without regard to degrees of unacceptability.

- ◆ *Number of points on the scale.* If a scoring rubric is constructed with six, seven, or eight points, then the placement of the "unacceptable" line might be different than for a rubric with only four points. A five-point scale (while not ideal from the standpoint of having an odd number of points) allows two levels of unacceptable while also permitting finer degrees of excellence, with the upper levels representing, for example, barely acceptable, good, and excellent.

- ◆ *Developmental vs. non-developmental rubrics.* Clearly, for a developmental rubric that defines performance over an extended period of time, there is no need to define the distinction between acceptable and unacceptable performance in the same manner as for a performance-specific rubric. In this case, judgments as to acceptability and expectations do not reside in the rubric, but in the use that is made of them in different settings.

Titles for Levels of Performance

Closely related to the need to define the cut-off between acceptable and unacceptable performance is the requirement to broadly define the labels for each point on the rubric. Teachers often use words such as "unacceptable" and "exemplary." Although such descriptions might work even if students (or their families) will see the rubric, such descriptions should be given some thought. Some educators prefer designations like "novice," "emerging," "proficient," and "distinguished." Decisions as to the best headings are matters for professional judgment and consensus. Naturally, it's possible to simply use numbers (1, 2, 3, etc.) without implying judgment.

Descriptions of Performance

Descriptions for levels of performance should be written in language that is truly descriptive rather than comparative. For example, words such as "average" should be avoided, as in "the number of computational errors is average," and replaced by statements such as "the solution contains only minor computational errors." "Minor" will then have to be defined, as, for example, "an error not resulting in an erroneous conclusion," or "an error that was clearly based in carelessness." In this case, it's not the number of errors but the type of mistakes that make a difference in the level of performance.

Generic vs. Task-Specific

Constructing a performance rubric for student work takes considerable time, particularly if it is a joint effort among many educators. The issue of time, and the desire to send a consistent signal to students and their families regarding standards, are important reasons to try to create generic rubrics. Such rubrics may be used for many different specific tasks that students do.

The areas of student performance that appear to lend themselves best to generic rubrics are such things as math journals, problem solving tasks, expository (or descriptive, or argument) essays, and oral presentations. Some of these, for example, oral presentations, are suitable for several different disciplines. It is highly valuable for students to know, in a consistent manner, that when they are preparing an oral presentation, it will always be evaluated, in every situation, and in every course at the secondary level, using the same criteria.

However, generic rubrics are not always possible, or even desirable. The elements of problem solving, and certainly the levels of acceptable performance, are very different for high school sophomores than for second graders. So while there are many reasons to construct rubrics that are as generic as possible—intra- and cross-departmental discussions are highly recommended—it may not be possible to develop completely generic rubrics, There are many types of tasks that require their own, task-specific rubric.

Professional Consensus

When teachers work together to determine descriptions of levels of performance in a scoring rubric, they may find that they do not completely agree. This is natural and to be expected. After all, it is well-documented that teachers grade student work quite differently from one another.

Discussions about the proper wording for different levels of performance constitute rich professional experiences. While difficult, the discussions are generally enriching for everyone involved; most teachers find that their ideas can be enhanced by the contributions of their colleagues. Rubrics that are the product of many minds are generally superior to those created by individuals. In addition, if a number of teachers find that they can use the same, or similar, rubrics for evaluating student work, communication with students is that much more consistent, resulting in better quality work from students.

Inter-Rater Agreement

Closely related to reaching consensus on the descriptions of performance levels is the matter of agreement on the rubric's application. The only way to be sure that there is agreement on the meaning of the descriptions of different levels is to apply the statements to samples of student work.

The importance of this issue cannot be emphasized enough. It is a fundamental principle of equity and fairness that evaluation of a student's work be the same regardless of who is doing the evaluating. However, teachers rarely agree completely at the beginning. Occasionally, two teachers will evaluate a single piece of student work very differently, even when they have agreed on the scoring rubric. In those cases, they generally discover that they were interpreting words in the rubric differently, or that the words used were themselves ambiguous. Only by trying the rubric with actual student work are such difficulties revealed.

When preparing rubrics for evaluating student work, therefore, the project is not totally complete until examples of different levels of performance are selected to illustrate the points on the scale. Called "anchor papers," these samples serve to maintain consistency in scoring.

Clarity of Directions

Another fundamental principle of fairness and equity concerns the directions given to students. Any criterion to be evaluated must be clearly asked for in the directions to a performance task. For example, if students are to be evaluated on their originality in making an oral presentation, something in the directions to them should recommend that they present it in an original or creative manner. Likewise, if students are to be evaluated on the organization of their data, they should know that organization is important. Otherwise, from a student's point of view, it is necessary to read the teacher's mind to guess what is important.

Some teachers even find that they can engage students in the development of the rubric itself. Students, they discover, know the indicators of a good oral presentation or of a well-solved problem. While students' thoughts are rarely well-enough organized to enable them to create a rubric on their own, their ideas make good additions to a teacher-drafted rubric.

There are many advantages to engaging students in the construction of a scoring rubric. Most obviously, they know what is included and can, therefore, focus their work. But even more importantly, students tend to do better work, with greater pride in it and with greater attention to its quality, when the evaluation criteria are clear. Suddenly, school is not a matter of "gotcha," it is a place where excellent work is both defined and expected.

Combining Scores on Criteria

Occasionally, it is important to combine scores on different criteria and to arrive at a single evaluation. For example, teachers must occasionally rank students, or convert their judgments on performance to a grade or to a percentage. How can this be done?

In arriving at a single, holistic score, several issues must be addressed:

- ◆ *Weight.* Are all the criteria of equal importance? Unless one or another is designated as more or less important than the others, they should all be assumed to be of equal importance. Educators should have good reasons for their decisions as to weight, and these discussions can themselves constitute important professional conversations. As an example, when creating the server rubric, we could have determined that "knowledge" is the most important criterion and that it is worth twice the value of the others. Then, our rubric, and the points possible from each point, would appear as shown in Table 6.3.
- ◆ *Calculations.* How should the scores be calculated? Clearly, the easiest technique is to convert the assigned scores on each criterion, as reflected in the weights assigned to each criterion, to a percentage of the total possible number of points, using a formula similar to this:

52 ◆ Using Rubrics to Evaluate Complex Performance

Score Assigned × Weight = Criterion Score
Criterion Score on Each Criterion = Total Score
Total Score/Total Possible Scores = Percentage Score

Table 6.3 Weighted Server Rubric

Name: <u>Jamie Jones</u>   Restaurant: <u>Hilltop Cafe</u>

	Level One	Level Two	Level Three	Level Four
Courtesy Weight = 1		X		
Appearance Weight = 1				X
Responsiveness Weight = 1			X	
Knowledge Weight = 2	X			
Coordination Weight = 1				X
Accuracy Weight = 1			X	

Using this procedure for Jamie Jones, her point score is:

Courtesy:	2 (2 × 1)
Appearance:	4 (4 × 1)
Responsiveness:	3 (3 × 1)
Knowledge:	2 (1 × 2)
Coordination:	4 (4 × 1)
Accuracy:	3 (3 × 1)
Total:	18

On this rubric, the maximum possible score for each criterion is:

Courtesy:	4
Appearance:	4
Responsiveness:	4
Knowledge:	8

Responsiveness:	4
Accuracy:	4
Total:	28

Thus, in our example, Jamie Jones received a score of 18 which, when divided by 28, is 64%.

- ◆ *Cut score.* What is the overall level of acceptable performance? We defined earlier the line between acceptable and unacceptable performance for each criterion. However, we must now determine a score which, overall, represents acceptable performance. We could set it as a percentage, for example 70%, in which case Jamie Jones would not be hired in our restaurant. Alternatively, we could establish a rule that no more than one criterion may be rated below three. This decision, like all the others made in constructing a performance rubric, is a matter of professional judgment.

Time

Not only for large-scale assessment, but also in the classroom, teachers know that multiple choice, short-answer, matching, and true/false tests take far less time to score than essay or open-ended tests. It is a relatively simple matter to take a stack of student tests and grade them against an answer key. Many educators fear that using performance tasks and rubrics will consume more time than they have or want to devote to it.

There is some validity to this concern. It is true that the evaluation of student work using a rubric takes more time than does grading student tests against a key. And the rubric itself can take considerable time to create.

However, there are two important issues to consider. One relates to the increasing ease of using performance tasks, and the second relates to the benefits derived from their use.

- ◆ *Decreasing time demands.* When they are just beginning to use performance tasks and rubrics, many teachers find that the time requirements are far greater than those needed for traditional tests. However, as they become more skilled, and as the rubrics they have developed prove to be useful for other assignments or other types of work, teachers discover that they can evaluate student work efficiently and, in many cases, in very little more time, if any, than that required for traditional tests.
- ◆ *Other benefits.* Most teachers discover that the benefits derived from increased use of performance tasks and rubrics vastly outweigh the

additional time needed. They discover that students produce better quality work and that students take greater pride in that work. When performance tasks and rubrics are used as a component in assigning grades, teachers find that they can justify their decisions far more reliably than before they used rubrics.

Subjectivity vs. Objectivity

An important reservation about the use of rubrics to evaluate student work concerns their perceived "subjectivity" when compared to the "objectivity" of multiple-choice tests. Such fears, while understandable, are unjustified.

First, it is important to remember that the only objective feature to a multiple-choice test is its scoring; answers are unambiguously right or wrong. However, many professional judgments have entered into making the test itself, and even into determining which of the possible answers is the correct one. Someone must decide what questions to ask and how to structure the problems. These decisions reflect a vision of what are the important knowledge and skill for students to demonstrate, and are based on professional judgment.

Similarly, in the construction of a scoring rubric, many decisions must be made. These, too, are made on the basis of professional judgment. But the fact that they are made by teachers in their classrooms, rather than by testing companies, does not make them less valid judgments. It may be argued that, if well thought out, such judgments are superior to those made by anonymous agencies far from the realities of one's own classroom.

In any event, both scoring rubrics to evaluate student work and standardized tests are grounded in professional judgment. They are absolutely equivalent on that score. In both cases, it is the quality of the judgments that is important, and the classroom-based judgment may be as good as that made by the testing company.

Chapter Summary

◆ Rubrics are complex and rigorous tools for evaluating complex performance.

◆ Rubrics of high quality are a result of many factors, including the appropriateness of the number and titles of levels or performance, the match between the type of rubric bring used to the performance being evaluated, and the dividing line between acceptable and unacceptable performance.

◆ Analytic rubrics can be used to evaluate student work on multiple, independent criteria. However, they can also be used to generate holistic scores of student work. Generating holistic scores with rubrics sometimes requires weighting to ensure more important components of performance factor more heavily into a final score.

☑ Professional Development Tip

Analyzing Rubrics

One way to begin to familiarize yourself with rubrics is to engage in an analysis of several examples. A mix of quality, vetted rubrics and those that result from an internet search can provide a good supply to begin the review. A good place to begin collect rubrics is your state department of education. Generally, they publish samples of rubrics used to evaluate work from end-of-course or annual examinations. These are good to use as a reference, as they also reflect the standard to which students' work is held on these examinations. Additionally, curriculum publishers often include a variety of generic and specific rubrics to which you should refer in your search.

Each participant in the session should receive several sample rubrics (preferably without the source information included), and should analyze the following aspects of each rubric:

◆ What criteria does the rubric measure? Are some criteria more heavily weighted than others in a scoring formula?

◆ How many performance levels are there? (Are there an odd or even number?) What are they titled? Do they use supportive, positive titles for each performance level?

◆ Where is the dividing line between acceptable and unacceptable performance?

◆ Is this a generic or task-specific rubric? Is it a holistic, analytic or developmental rubric?

◆ Is the language used in the rubric clear? Does it require further definition/ explanation (e.g., the "minor" error example above)?

Reviewing the rubrics for these elements can help familiarize participating teachers with elements that are useful for judging quality. Additional review can focus on the elements of the rubric that are useful when evaluating student work. Professional conversations about the utility of the rubric as well as the elements of performance evaluated by the rubric can be invaluable as teachers refine their understanding of the types of rubrics and criteria for judging their quality.

7

Creating and Adapting Rubrics

Developing a rubric is no small feat. With experience—teaching the same grade level or course over the course of several years, for instance—teachers come to understand how students' understandings develop and the common errors and misconceptions that may be exhibited in students' work. However, it is easy to underestimate the challenge of identifying what students must show in their work to be considered proficient. Similarly, there are many ways in which students can fall short of the proficient bar. The development of the task and the application of the rubric should be considered an iterative process (as each is developed and used, it suggests changes in the other) with the final combination of task and rubric evolving over time. This section includes guidance for the design of a rubric for a task.

Drafting a Scoring Rubric

Generally speaking, the criteria to be used in evaluating student work will have been identified in the course of developing a performance task. They should reflect the standards and learning goals being assessed by the performance task. However, in order to convert these criteria into an actual scoring rubric, they must be elaborated and further defined. As described in Chapter 6, there are two main types of rubrics, holistic and analytic. Holistic rubrics are designed to capture the overall quality of a student's performance on the task. Analytic rubrics, on the other hand, break down performance into multiple dimensions. Each dimension is then elaborated and defined across multiple levels of performance. While holistic rubrics have their uses (e.g., in the summative evaluation of student work for awarding a diploma), this section will focus on the design of analytic rubrics.

Generic or Task-Specific?

The first question to be answered concerns the degree of task-specificity of the rubric. If, for example, the rubric is being developed for a group mathematics project, could the same rubric be used for other projects, or is its use confined to this particular one? Indeed, could the elements of the rubric, concerned with making a group presentation, be used for other disciplines as well? Are there enough similarities between group presentations for mathematics, science, and social studies that the same evaluation guide could be used for all of them? In addition to the application to different types of performances (e.g., individual versus group), different disciplines, generic rubrics can be most valuable when applied across performances as a tool for assessing students' growth. For example, a generic rubric could be used to assess students' ability to solve multistep multiplication and division word problems across a school year (or multiple school years).

Table 7.1 Performance Rubric (Activity)

Criteria	1	2	3	4

In general, of course, generic rubrics are more useful that task-specific ones. Creating rubrics is time-consuming and the more broadly they may be applied, the more useful and powerful they are. However, sometimes a generic rubric will have to be adapted when the ways in which elements appear in student work are sufficiently different to warrant independent consideration.

Task- or Genre-Specific, or Developmental?

Another important question to be considered when creating a rubric is whether the rubric will be used on a single task (or a single type of task) or whether it will be used developmentally with students as they progress

58 ◆ Creating and Adapting Rubrics

through many years of school. That is, will the rubric under development for a mathematics project be applied for only this particular project which students do in the seventh grade, or could it be used also with students throughout the district, including those in the elementary school as well as in high school?

If the rubric is to be used developmentally, it will probably have many more points on its scale, and the criteria may be written differently than if the rubric is to be used for a single task. A developmental rubric is useful for a school in which students have mathematics portfolios, and may be helpful in charting progress over time. However, a developmental rubric may not be as useful for any particular task as one created specifically for that task.

Determining Criteria

Once the question of whether to develop a task-specific or generic rubric has been answered, the most important single step in creating a scoring rubric is to identify the criteria to be evaluated. The importance of attending carefully to this step cannot be overstated. It is in the determination of criteria that educators define important aspects of performance, and define, both for themselves and their students, what they mean by good quality. When defining criteria, several issues should be considered.

◆ *Type of criteria.* In mathematics, an essential criterion almost always concerns mathematical accuracy. Is the answer correct? Are computational errors major or minor? Are answers correctly labeled? Are all possible answers found?

But in addition to computational accuracy, what else is important? What about conceptual understanding? Do students reveal, either through their approach to the problem or through the errors they make, that they have good understanding of the underlying concepts? Does the problem require a plan? If so, have students organized their information? Have they approached the problem in a systematic manner? Can a reader follow the student's line of reasoning?

In addition, a mathematics project might require that students collaborate with one another. How successfully do they do this? Do they establish an equitable division of labor, or do one or two students dominate the group? If the students make a presentation as part of the project, do they explain their thinking clearly? Are the other students interested in the presentation? Can they follow it? Is it engaging? It is important that the criteria identified for a task not consist only of those that are easiest to see, such as computational accuracy. The criteria should, taken together, define all the aspects of exemplary performance, even if some of them are somewhat challenging to specify and to evaluate.

One successful approach to the identification of criteria is to consider the task and to imagine an excellent student response to it. What would such a response include? The answer to that question can serve to identify important criteria. It is recommended that teachers do the task themselves prior to assigning it to their students, creating, in effect, an exemplary response, and appreciating the issues inherent in the task for students.

- *Number and detail of criteria.* There is no single best answer to the question of "how many criteria?" Clearly, all important aspects of performance should be captured in the criteria. Moreover, those aspects of performance that are independent of one another should be designated as separate criteria.

  It is possible to designate too many criteria, and for them to be too detailed. The resulting rubric is then cumbersome and time-consuming to use. On the other hand, a rubric that is too economical may not provide adequate information to students for them to improve performance or for teachers to use in helping students improve. The number and level of detail of the rubric then, is partly a matter of how it is to be used and the age and skill level of the students. Rubrics used with students with special needs, for example, are often made in great detail, so both teachers and students are aware of where improvement efforts should be focused.

- *Sub-criteria or elements.* Sometimes, several criteria are related to one another or one may be considered a sub-category of another. In that case, the criteria may contain within them sub-criteria or elements. For example, if students make a presentation as part of the mathematics project, the overall criterion might be "quality of presentation" with sub-criteria of "clarity," "originality and energy," and "involvement of all group members."

  Occasionally, when educators think critically about the qualities they would look for in good student performance, they recognize that the task, as written, does not elicit those qualities; they then return to the task and alter the student directions. That is, students could do the task and not demonstrate the criteria that have been defined. In that case, the directions must be rewritten, or the task restructured, to elicit the desired performance.

Number of Points

Critical to the design of rubrics in the number of points used to evaluate each criterion. One important design consideration not to be overlooked: as mentioned in Chapter 6, an even number is preferable to an odd number, since it prevents the phenomenon known as "central tendency." But beyond that, there are several considerations to keep in mind.

- *Detail in distinctions.* With a larger number of points on a scale, fine distinctions are required when evaluating student work. While such detail can provide finely-tuned feedback to students and information for teachers, a rubric with many points is difficult to write and cumbersome and time-consuming to use. For practical purposes, a rubric with 4–6 points is recommended. The tasks in this collection all contain 4 points.
- *Dividing line between acceptable and unacceptable performance.* It is helpful, at the outset, to determine the dividing line between acceptable and unacceptable performance. On a 4-point scale, this line is either between the "1" and the "2" or between the "2" and the "3." That placement will be determined by where the greater detail is the more useful; that is, is it more useful to be able to specify degrees of inadequacy or degrees of adequacy?
- *General headings for different points.* The different points on the scale may be called simply by their numbers. On a 4-point scale then, they would be 0, 1, 2, and 3 or 1, 2, 3, and 4. Or, they could be 10, 20, 30, and 40. Alternatively, the points can be given names such as "novice," "emerging," "proficient," and "exemplary." If this approach is taken, it is preferable to use positive, supportive words (such as "emerging") rather than negative ones (such as "inadequate").

Descriptions of Levels of Performance

Once the criteria and the number of scale points have been determined, it is time to actually write the descriptions of performance levels. Again, this step is critical and includes a number of factors.

- *The language used.* The words used to specify the qualities of different levels of performance should be descriptive, rather than comparative. For example, words such as "average" should be avoided. The descriptions of performance levels serve to further define the criteria, and are further defined themselves only when accompanied by actual samples of student work, called anchor papers. When describing the qualities of lower levels of performance, it is important to include elements that will exist in the work alongside things that are missing. So, for example, rather than defining emerging performance as merely, "unable to solve multistep word problems involving multiplication and division," a rubric would better serve its users if it defined emerging performance as, "able to solve single-step word problems involving multiplication and division."

◆ *All sub-criteria or elements defined.* If the criteria contain sub-criteria within them, each of these elements should be described in each of the performance descriptions. For example, if a criterion on presentation includes accuracy and originality, and involvement of all group members, then the descriptions for each of the levels should describe the group's presentation with respect to all those elements. This parallel rubric structure enables teachers to more easily evaluate performance on sub-criteria and provide clear feedback to students.

◆ *Distance between points.* To the extent possible, the distance between the points on a scale should be equal. That is, the distance between a "3" and a "4" should not be much greater than that between a "2" and a "3."

◆ *Defining proficiency.* Placement of the line between acceptable (proficient) and unacceptable performance should receive particular scrutiny. While the highest and lowest levels of performance are the easiest to describe, those in the middle, which define acceptable and unacceptable performance, are the most important. It is here, after all, that educators define their standards and specify the quality of work on which they insist and expect mastery. It is recommended that this level be described with particular care. And it is often best to start describing performance with the "proficient" level of performance, e.g., 3 points on a 4-point scale. When articulating this performance level, consider

– Content standards, specifically the concepts or skills students should understand or be able to use.
– Standards for Mathematical Practice, also described as habits of mind, mathematical process standards, etc. These reflect the kinds of behaviors proficient students engage in. The Common Core State Standards for Mathematics define eight of these standards, including the ability of students to model

62 ◆ Creating and Adapting Rubrics

mathematically and look for and make use of the structure observed in a problem or their own work.
- Other affective skills demanded or required. For instance, are students required to collaborate as part of a group or team for this project?

Piloting the Rubric with Student Work

A rubric's purpose is in the evaluation of student work, and not until a rubric is used to evaluate actual student work will its authors know whether it is viable. Several steps are recommended.

Evaluating a Sample of Student Work

A good place to begin is to collect a small number of samples (about 8) of students' work, representing the full range of probable responses in the class. The sample should include those students from whom the best work would be expected, as well as those whose work might not be adequate. If possible, the pieces of work should be anonymous; they could be numbered and referred to by their numbers.

Then, with the rubric in hand, evaluate the student work using the draft rubric. The form shown in Table 7.2 may be used, with the criteria listed (or numbered) down the side, and the levels of performance for different

Table 7.2 Performance Assessment Evaluation Results

Evaluator _____ Date _____

Task _____ Grade Level _____

Criteria	Student 1	Student 2	Student 3	Student 4

students specified in the column corresponding to each one. Surveying the entire page then provides a summary of the levels of performance represented by the class as a whole, and can offer guidance as to the next instructional steps that may be needed.

Inter-Rater Agreement

Even with careful design, it is possible that the rubric or the use of the rubric is not yet reliable. Unfortunately, educators often use education terminology with loosely defined meanings, such as rigor, understanding, etc. Or teachers, as colleagues, have dissonant expectations for student work. Addressing the potential lack of inter-rater agreement requires assistance from a colleague. It is recommended that another educator be introduced to the task and the rubric, and be provided with the same sample of student work initially used. This person should then evaluate the same students, and assign scores on each criterion based on the draft rubric.

Scores for each student on each criterion should then be compared. Clearly, the goal is for all scores to be the same, although this is unlikely to occur. Any discrepancies should then be discussed until the cause of the discrepancy is understood; most frequently, discrepancies are caused by a lack of clarity in the words used in the performance levels.

☑ **Professional Development Tip**

Setting Up Collaborative Sessions to Score Student Work

Teacher collaboration in the scoring of student work using a rubric (whether self-designed or part of a commercial program) offers a great opportunity for professional development. In addition to providing feedback to refine the design of the rubric, this activity provides teachers with an opportunity to

◆ Develop shared definitions of language and terminology.

◆ Bring differences in expectations for student performance to light and engage teachers in professional dialogue to address those differences.

◆ Share ideas on how to provide feedback to students.

(continued)

> *(continued)*
>
> Collaborative scoring sessions can easily be set up among teachers at a grade level. Teachers can begin by selecting several pieces of work at each of the performance levels. Then they can give that work to colleagues to score and compare ratings along with their rationales. Alternatively, teachers can use the rubric along with a small set of student work samples and use a protocol to look carefully at 4 pieces of student work. Each teacher might bring work about which they have questions or which doesn't fit neatly into one of the performance levels. The protocol could involve a descriptive review (in which low-inference evidence is collected) followed by an analysis of that evidence in which it is aligned to the criteria and performance levels of the rubric. The heart of the professional learning experience is the professional discourse that emerges as colleagues address ambiguity, uncertainty, disagreement, etc.

Revising the Rubric (and Possibly the Task)

As a result of evaluating student work and of comparing scores assigned with those of another educator, it is likely that the rubric (and possibly also the task) will require some revision. With luck, these revisions will not be extensive and will serve to clarify points of ambiguity.

Locating Anchor Papers

As a final step in rubric design, samples of student work that represent different points on the scale on each of the different criteria should be identified. By keeping these from year to year, it is possible to chart the course of general improvement of student work over time. In addition, only through the use of anchor papers can educators be sure that their standards are remaining the same, and are not subject to a gradual drift.

Involving Students in Rubric Design and Use

Many educators find that one of the most powerful uses of performance tasks and rubrics is to engage students actively in their design and use. That aspect of work with rubrics is described in this section, which may be used productively even with elementary students.

Advantages

Many advantages are cited for engaging students in the design of scoring rubrics. First and most important, by participating in the design of a scoring rubric, students are absolutely clear on the criteria by which their work will be evaluated. Furthermore, many teachers discover that students have good ideas to contribute to a rubric; they know, for example, the characteristics of an exemplary mathematics project.

But more importantly, when students know at the outset the criteria by which their work will be evaluated, and when they know the description of exemplary performance, they are better able (and more motivated) to produce high-quality work. The rubric provides guidance as to quality; students know exactly what they must do.

Consequently, many teachers find that when they involve students in the use of scoring rubrics, the quality of student work improves dramatically. So, when teachers have anchors (e.g., exemplary projects from a previous year) to illustrate good quality work to students, the general standard of work produced improves from year to year.

A Plan for Action

It is not obvious just how to engage students in designing and using scoring rubrics for evaluating student work. Some suggestions are offered here.

◆ *Starting with a draft.* A discussion with students about scoring rubrics should begin with a draft rubric already prepared by the teacher. The teacher should have some ideas, at least in general terms, of the criteria that should emerge from the discussion. Then, while students may suggest original ideas, the teacher can be sure that the final product includes all important aspects of performance. Another approach involves sharing the proficient criteria on the rubric for students. Students can they work to help define what additional criteria would be required for work to be considered exemplary. Similarly, they can help in defining the criteria for the lowest point on the scale. The distinction between the near-proficient and proficient levels of performance is often the hardest to make, and students would likely have the most difficulty defining it.

Students may also be asked to contribute both to the generation of criteria and to the writing of performance descriptions. Many teachers are pleasantly surprised with the level of sophistication demonstrated by their students in this endeavor.

The teacher should maintain control of the process of rubric design. While students will have excellent ideas, which should be accommodated to the maximum extent possible, the teacher should never relinquish control of the project to students.

66 ◆ Creating and Adapting Rubrics

- *Student self-assessment.* The first type of student use of a scoring rubric might be for students to evaluate their own work. Most teachers find that their students are, generally speaking, quite hard on themselves, in some cases more so than their teachers would be. Of course, clear performance descriptions will help in keeping evaluations consistent, but students frequently reveal a genuine concern for maintaining high standards, even when evaluating their own work. Task-specific rubrics that include expectations that reflect the demands of the performance task are less appropriate for students to use because they often include answers or strategies embedded as "look fors" in the rubric.
- *Peer assessment.* When the climate in a class is sufficiently supportive, students may be able to engage in peer assessment. Such an activity requires a high level of trust among students. However, if students have participated in the design of a scoring rubric, and have used it to evaluate their own work, they will generally be able to provide feedback to their peers in the same spirit of caring and support. When that occurs, the classroom becomes transformed into a true community of learners.

Adapting Existing Rubrics

Frequently, adapting an existing scoring rubric to one's own use may save much time and effort. Through this approach, educators can benefit from the work of others, and still have a rubric that reflects their own specific needs.

There are many sources of existing rubrics that may be adapted, in addition to those in this book. Many textbook publishers now offer some rubrics as part of their package. Some state departments of education and the National Council of Teachers of Mathematics (NCTM) have also created prototype rubrics. And with the widespread adoption of the Common Core State Standards, there are many tasks and accompanying rubrics available that are aligned to the standards used by teachers across the country.

Adapting the Criteria
When adapting rubrics, it is critical to ensure that the criteria apply to the task being assessed. Begin by asking

- ◆ What knowledge, skills, and understandings are required by the task?
- ◆ What dispositions, habits of mind, or practices do you expect students to demonstrate in performing the task? How will you measure them?
- ◆ What does the rubric offer to me as a user? How closely is it aligned with the objectives I have articulated for the task and my students?

One pitfall to be avoided is altering expectations of student work in response to a performance task to conform to a rubric. If the task encourages students to exhibit knowledge, skill, or understanding that are not reflected in the rubric, criteria related to these features should be added. Alternatively, if the rubric demands that students demonstrate knowledge, skill, or understanding unlikely to be exhibited in students' work, the criteria corresponding to those elements should be eliminated.

Adjusting the Performance Descriptions

Depending on the expectations and the particular task being assessed, the performance descriptions of a rubric may require adjustment. For example, using a rubric designed for a different grade or a previous set of standards may require adjustments in the descriptions of performance levels. Additionally, adoption of new standards may alter the definition of proficiency and, hence, the dividing line between acceptable and unacceptable performance.

Understanding an Adapted Rubric

When adapting a rubric, rather than developing it from scratch, it's important to be sure to work collaboratively to understand the expectations of the rubric. There are two key steps teachers can take to help ensure inter-rater agreement and consistent and fair use of a rubric, which are:

- ◆ Collaborate with colleagues to rewrite performance descriptions, where necessary. This can also be done with the goal of writing the descriptions in a student-friendly format. This has the added benefit of a version of the rubric that can clearly communicate your expectations with students. It also helps to clarify jargon, or overly vague language, as described earlier in this book.
- ◆ Apply the rubric to samples of student work from the task you intend to use it with.

68 ◆ Creating and Adapting Rubrics

When adopting or adapting a rubric, keep in mind that it should reflect your values and expectations. While good rubrics have the potential to change thinking about assessment, a thoughtfully designed task should not be compromised by a rubric designed for a different task or a different set of standards.

Piloting a Rubric with Students

Does the scoring rubric, as revised, still meet all the technical requirements described in Chapter 6? Do the descriptions of levels of performance use vivid words, and avoid comparative language? Are the distances between points on the scale approximately equal? Do the criteria reflect the most important aspects of performance?

Only an actual pilot of the revised task will elicit unambiguous answers to these questions. As educators and their students become more experienced in the use of performance tasks, however, this step may be combined with the first actual use of the task to evaluate student learning. That is, the task may be adapted as needed and used with students. Then, if it becomes apparent that the adaptation did not avoid all the pitfalls described above, the actual scores awarded to students can be adjusted accordingly. For example, if student performance is poor, but it becomes clear that the principal reason for the poor performance relates to lack of clarity in the directions, then the teacher's evaluation of student mastery must reflect that difficulty.

Chapter Summary

◆ Rubrics are complex instruments designed to evaluate complex performance. When designing or adapting rubrics, many factors must be considered. A critical step is the initial design of a rubric. For this process, a number of factors—such as whether it is generic or specific, the actual criteria, the number of points on the scale, and the language used to define the points—must be taken into account

◆ The number of points used to evaluate each criterion should, whenever possible, be an even number and contain enough points to meaningfully distinguish between levels of performance while not too many that it becomes time-consuming for teachers to use. Identifying the line between acceptable and unacceptable performance is a critical task when creating a rubric.

◆ Not until a scoring rubric has been piloted with actual student papers will its designers know whether it will prove to be effective. Collecting anchor papers that represent the actual work described in the rubric will ensure that the rubric can be applied fairly and reliably.

8

Middle School Mathematics Performance Tasks

In this section of the book you will find a collection of performance tasks and rubrics aligned to the mathematics standards, and addressing important topics in middle school mathematics. They are arranged in alphabetical order (by title), with a table at the beginning of the chapter to assist you in locating tasks you may want to use to assess specific skills and concepts. Some of the tasks include student work, which serves both to illustrate the manner in which students interpret the directions given to them and to anchor the different points in the scoring rubrics.

You may find that the tasks are useful to you as presented. Alternatively, you may find that they can serve your purposes better if you adapt them somewhat. One way of adapting tasks is to incorporate names of people and places familiar to students in your class. This practice is frequently amusing to students, and therefore engaging.

In addition, tasks may be simplified or made more difficult by increasing or decreasing the amount of structure (or scaffolding) you provide to students. When you, the teacher, give guidance to students by outlining the steps needed in a solution, the resulting task is significantly easier (and less authentic). Similarly, for those tasks that are provided with considerable scaffolding, you can make them more complex by removing it.

The rubrics presented in this book include criteria across three major dimensions of performance, namely a student's

- ◆ problem solving approach;
- ◆ accuracy and procedural skill; and
- ◆ ability to communicate his or her mathematical ideas, understandings, and work.

These three complementary dimensions are designed to provide teachers with a comprehensive picture and understanding of students' mathematical understanding and skill. "Problem solving approach" refers to students' ability to make sense of a problem and select a strategy and implement it, or reason about how to solve the problem. "Accuracy and procedural skill" collectively refer to students' procedural and computational skill. This dimension also includes key elements of precision identified in the Common Core State Standards for Mathematical Practice, including labeling units and using precise mathematical language. Lastly, we assess students' "communication." Many of the performance tasks in this collection explicitly ask that students explain their thinking. In doing so, we ask them to engage in and demonstrate an important skill that extends well beyond mathematics. Can a student explain her reasoning? Can she help someone else better understand her ideas? Together, these three large dimensions are used by teachers seeking to gain insight into students' knowledge, understanding, skills, and behaviors as those students pose and solve mathematical problems.

Table 8.1 Middle School Tasks Alignment Chart

Task Name	Grade Level	Common Core Content Standards	Common Core Standards for Mathematical Practice
All in a Day	6	6.RP Understand ratio concepts and use ratio reasoning to solve problems. 5.MD.2 Represent and Interpret Data.	SMP1 Make sense of problems and persevere in solving them. SMP2 Reason abstractly and quantitatively. SMP4 Model with mathematics.
Arcade Accounting	7–8	7SP Investigate chance processes and develop, use, and evaluate probability models. 7EE Apply and extend previous understandings of operations with fractions to add, subtract, multiply, and divide rational numbers.	SMP1 Make sense of problems and persevere in solving them. SMP2 Reason abstractly and quantitatively. SMP4 Model with mathematics.
Basketball Camp	6	6.NS Compute fluently with multi-digit numbers.	SMP1 Make sense of problems and persevere in solving them. SMP2 Reason abstractly and quantitatively. SMP4 Model with mathematics.
Bull's Eye	7	6.G Solve real-world and mathematical problems involving area, surface area, and volume. 7.G Know the formulas for the area and circumference of a circle. 7SP Investigate chance processes and develop, use, and evaluate probability models.	SMP1 Make sense of problems and persevere in solving them. SMP2 Reason abstractly and quantitatively. SMP4 Model with mathematics.

(continued)

Table 8.1 *(continued)*

Task Name	Grade Level	Common Core Content Standards	Common Core Standards for Mathematical Practice
Chalk It Up	6–7	6.RP Understand ratio concepts and use ratio reasoning to solve problems. 6.G Solve real world and mathematical problems involving area, surface area, and volume.	SMP1 Make sense of problems and persevere in solving them. SMP2 Reason abstractly and quantitatively. SMP4 Model with mathematics. SMP6 Attend to precision.
Checkers Tournament	7	7SP Investigate chance processes and develop, use, and evaluate probability models.	SMP1 Make sense of problems and persevere in solving them. SMP2 Reason abstractly and quantitatively. SMP4 Model with mathematics. SMP7 Look for and make use of structure.
Country Mile	6–7	6.G Solve real-world and mathematical problems involving area, surface area, and volume. 7.EE Solve real world problems using numerical and algebraic expressions and equations. 7.G Know the formulas for the area and circumference of a circle. 7.NS Apply and extend previous understandings of operations with fractions to add, subtract, multiply, and divide rational numbers.	SMP1 Make sense of problems and persevere in solving them. SMP2 Reason abstractly and quantitatively. SMP4 Model with mathematics.

Eeny, Meeny, Miny, Moe	6–7	6NS. Apply and extend previous understanding of multiplication and division. 7.NS Apply and extend previous understandings of operations with fractions to add, subtract, multiply, and divide rational numbers.	SMP1 Make sense of problems and persevere in solving them. SMP2 Reason abstractly and quantitatively. SMP4 Model with mathematics. SMP6 Attend to Precision SMP7 Look for and make use of structure.
Hollywood Stars	8	8.G Understand congruence and similarity using physical models, transparencies, or geometry software. 8.F The graph of a function is the set of ordered pairs consisting of an input and the corresponding output.[1]	SMP1 Make sense of problems and persevere in solving them. SMP2 Reason abstractly and quantitatively. SMP4 Model with mathematics. SMP6 Attend to precision.
Lineup	7	7SP Investigate chance processes and develop, use, and evaluate probability models.	SMP1 Make sense of problems and persevere in solving them. SMP2 Reason abstractly and quantitatively. SMP3 Construct viable arguments. SMP4 Model with mathematics. SMP7 Look for and make use of structure.

(continued)

Table 8.1 *(continued)*

Task Name	Grade Level	Common Core Content Standards	Common Core Standards for Mathematical Practice
Locker Combinations	7	7SP Investigate chance processes and develop, use, and evaluate probability models.	SMP1 Make sense of problems and persevere in solving them. SMP2 Reason abstractly and quantitatively. SMP3 Construct viable arguments. SMP4 Model with mathematics. SMP7 Look for and make use of structure.
Lucky Soda	6–7	6.NS Compute fluently with multi-digit numbers. 7SP Investigate chance processes and develop, use, and evaluate probability models.	SMP1 Make sense of problems and persevere in solving them. SMP2 Reason abstractly and quantitatively. SMP3 Construct viable arguments. SMP4 Model with mathematics. SMP7 Look for and make use of structure.
Lunch Menu	6–7	7.SP.2 Use random sampling to draw inferences about a population. 6.RP Understand ratio concepts and use ratio reasoning to solve problems.	SMP1 Make sense of problems and persevere in solving them. SMP3 Construct viable arguments and critique the reasoning of others. SMP4 Model with mathematics. SMP6 Attend to precision.

Money From Trash	6–7	6.NS Compute fluently with multi-digit numbers.	SMP1 Make sense of problems and persevere in solving them. SMP2 Reason abstractly and quantitatively. SMP3 Construct viable arguments. SMP4 Model with mathematics.
Outfits	6–7	6.NS Compute fluently with multi-digit numbers. 7SP Investigate chance processes and develop, use, and evaluate probability models.	SMP1 Make sense of problems and persevere in solving them. SMP2 Reason abstractly and quantitatively. SMP3 Construct viable arguments. SMP4 Model with mathematics. SMP7 Look for and make use of structure.
Pizza Party	6	6.NS Compute fluently with multi-digit numbers. 6.RP Understand ratio concepts and use ratio reasoning to solve problems.	SMP1 Make sense of problems and persevere in solving them. SMP2 Reason abstractly and quantitatively. SMP3 Construct viable arguments. SMP4 Model with mathematics.

(continued)

Table 8.1 *(continued)*

Task Name	Grade Level	Common Core Content Standards	Common Core Standards for Mathematical Practice
Planning a Playground	6	6.G Solve real-world and mathematical problems involving area, surface area, and volume.	SMP1 Make sense of problems and persevere in solving them. SMP2 Reason abstractly and quantitatively. SMP3 Construct viable arguments. SMP4 Model with mathematics.
Pool Pleasure	6–7	6.NS Compute fluently with multi-digit numbers. 6.RP Understand ratio concepts and use ratio reasoning to solve problems. 6.G Solve real-world and mathematical problems involving area, surface area, and volume. 7.EE Solve real world problems using numerical and algebraic expressions and equations.	SMP1 Make sense of problems and persevere in solving them. SMP2 Reason abstractly and quantitatively. SMP3 Construct viable arguments. SMP4 Model with mathematics.
Popcorn Estimation	6–7	6.NS Compute fluently with multi-digit numbers. 6.G Solve real world and mathematical problems involving area, surface area, and volume. 7.SP.2 Use random sampling to draw inferences about a population.	SMP1 Make sense of problems and persevere in solving them. SMP2 Reason abstractly and quantitatively. SMP3 Construct viable arguments. SMP4 Model with mathematics. SMP7 Look for and make use of structure.

Skydiving	6–7	6.G Solve real world and mathematical problems involving area, surface area, and volume. 7SP Investigate chance processes and develop, use, and evaluate probability models.	SMP1 Make sense of problems and persevere in solving them. SMP2 Reason abstractly and quantitatively. SMP4 Model with mathematics.
Spot	6–8	6.SP.5 Describe any overall pattern and any striking deviations from the overall pattern. 8.SP Investigate patterns of association in bivariate data.	SMP1 Make sense of problems and persevere in solving them. SMP2 Reason abstractly and quantitatively. SMP4 Model with mathematics. SMP7 Look for and make use of structure.
Traffic Lights	7–8	7SP Investigate chance processes and develop, use, and evaluate probability models.	SMP1 Make sense of problems and persevere in solving them. SMP2 Reason abstractly and quantitatively. SMP4 Model with mathematics. SMP7 Look for and make use of structure.
Unicycle Races		6.RP Use ratio and rate reasoning to solve real world and mathematical problems. 7.RP.1 Analyze proportional relationships and use them to solve real world problems.	SMP1 Make sense of problems and persevere in solving them. SMP3 Construct viable arguments and critique the reasoning of others. SMP4 Model with mathematics.
Variable Dilemma	7–8	7.EE Solve real life and mathematical problems using numerical and algebraic expressions and equations. 8.EE Analyze and solve linear equations.	SMP1 Make sense of problems and persevere in solving them. SMP2 Reason abstractly and quantitatively.

78 ◆ Middle School Mathematics Performance Tasks

ALL IN A DAY

Mathematics Assessed

- ◆ Number Operations and Concepts
- ◆ Geometry and Measurement
- ◆ Statistics and Probability
- ◆ Problem Solving and Mathematical Reasoning
- ◆ Mathematical Skills and Tools
- ◆ Mathematical Communication.

Directions to the Student

Make a graph to illustrate how many hours you spend on a typical school day involved in different types of activities. You should think about time sleeping, eating, being in school, doing homework, watching television, being with friends, playing sports, doing hobbies, etc.

You may want to make a table to organize your information, and you will have to select the best type of graph to use: for example, a bar graph, line graph, or circle graph. In addition, please show all your calculations and write a brief explanation of why you chose the graph you did and your method used in making the graph.

Materials Needed

- ◆ Graph paper
- ◆ Ruler
- ◆ Compass and protractor (for a circle graph)
- ◆ Calculator.

About This Task

This task asks students to collect, analyze, and communicate information through a graph, table, or chart. They must first design a simple data table, and calculate the number of hours spent in a typical day in each of the major activities. This activity will require that they estimate and calculate elapsed time. In addition, they should ensure that the number of hours in their "typical" day adds to 24 hours.

Next, students must select an appropriate graph or chart with which to communicate their results. A pictograph, a pie chart, and a bar graph are all suitable. A line graph would not be appropriate, since the events being graphed (sleeping, doing homework, eating, etc.) are discrete events; they are not continuous. For a pie chart, students will have to calculate the degrees of the circle represented by the different number of hours devoted to each activity.

Lastly, students must explain their method in writing. This narrative should reflect their estimation techniques, the reasons for their choice of graph type, and awareness that the sum of all the activities is 24 hours.

Solution

Answers will vary, depending on students' daily routine. A possible solution, with the proportionate number of degrees in a circle graph, is presented below:

Activity	Number of Hours	Degrees of a Circle
Eating	3 hours	45
Sleeping	8 hours	120
School	7 hours	105
Homework	2 hours	30
Bathing, dressing, etc.	2 hours	30
TV	2 hours	30
Total	24 hours	360

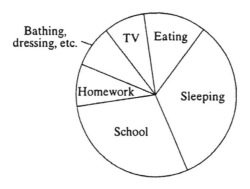

80 ◆ Middle School Mathematics Performance Tasks

Rubric

	Level One	Level Two	Level Three	Level Four
Problem Solving Approach	Graph chosen is inappropriate.	Graph chosen is appropriate, but not fully executed.	Graph is appropriate with adequate execution.	Graph is appropriate and well executed.
Accuracy and Procedural Skill	Solution is unsupported.	Solution is accurate but the computations do not fully support the solution.	Solution is accurate, with minor computational errors.	Solution is accurate, and the calculations demonstrate understanding of the structure of the problem.
Communication	Description is completely missing or inadequate. The student randomly presents information.	Description conveys some aspects of the method the student used for solving the problem, but is incomplete. The student attempts to organize the information; however it is incomplete or leads to errors.	Description adequately conveys a systematic method for solving the problem. The student organizes information in a fairly systematic manner.	Description clearly conveys an elegant and efficient method for solving the problem. In addition, the explanation reveals an understanding of the patterns inherent in the situation, e.g., how to solve similar problems. The student organizes information in an efficient and systematic manner.

Middle School Mathematics Performance Tasks ◆ 81

ARCADE ACCOUNTING

Mathematics Assessed

- Statistics and Probability Concepts
- Number and Operations Concepts
- Problem Solving and Mathematical Reasoning
- Mathematical Skills and Tools
- Mathematical Communication.

Directions to the Student

a. Liz, Rob, and Paul each have $7.50 to spend on their three favorite arcade games. The cost for playing each game is shown below. They decided to play each game the same number of times and then compared scores.

When they compared scores, they realized that Liz had more plays per game than Rob and Paul. Liz spent all of her money on the three games and played each game the greatest number of times possible. Rob and Paul spent all of their money too but did not get to play as many times as Liz.

How many times did Liz play each game? How many times might Rob and Paul play each game? Support your answers by showing how each person could have spent their money.

b. Liz says that if she had more money she would play the claw game with the cute plush toys.

Rob says he doesn't play the claw games because he doesn't think they are fair. He says that sometimes he can grab a toy but then the claw opens and the toy drops. They decide to do some

research on the claw game and find out that, by state regulation, the game is required to award a toy at least once every 10 games.

If a winning game occurs by random sometime during every consecutive set of 10 games, what is the probability that the first game of a set of 10 games will yield a prize? If the first game doesn't yield a prize what is the probability that the second game in the set will yield a prize? If the first 5 games in the set don't yield a prize what is the probability that the sixth game in the set will yield a prize? If the first 9 games in the set don't yield a prize what is the probability that the tenth game will yield a prize?

c. If it costs 50 cents to play the claw game and you can buy any of the toys for $3.00 at the toy store, would you take a chance at getting a toy by playing the game or by buying it at a toy store?

About This Task

In this task, students determine combinations of games that can be played with a given amount of money. They apply principles of probability to make a judgment about the wisdom of spending their money on a particular game at an arcade.

Solution

a. Liz plays each game 7 times by buying one single play and two triple plays or by buying two double plays and one triple play. Rob and Paul play each game 5 times by buying five single plays, or play each game 6 times by buying two single plays and two double plays.

b. The probability that the first game of a set of 10 games will yield a prize is 1/10. The probability that the second game yields a prize given that the first game did not yield a prize is 1/9. If the first 5 games in the set don't yield a prize, then the probability that the sixth game yields a prize is 1/5. If the first 9 games in the set don't yield a prize then the probability that the tenth game will yield a prize is 1/1 or a sure thing.

c. A student can make a case for playing or buying by citing probabilities from part b and by considering the best and worst case scenarios in terms of winning a toy by playing the game. In the best case scenario, they will win a toy at the first try which would only cost them $0.50 and under the worst case they would have to play more than 6 times to win a toy.

Rubric

	Level One	Level Two	Level Three	Level Four
Problem Solving Approach	Method used to solve the problem is disorganized, with no systematic method. Responses reveal little to no understanding of simple and conditional probability.	Method reveals some attempt at consistency, but not completely carried through. Responses reveal understanding of simple probability only.	Method is consistent, and if followed would yield correct solutions. Responses reveal some understanding of simple and conditional probability.	The method used is consistent and responses reveal understanding of simple and conditional probability.
Accuracy and Procedural Skill	Many errors in calculations, yielding wildly erroneous results.	Some computational inaccuracies, resulting in minor errors in the results.	Only minor errors in calculations; correct application of method.	No errors in computation; correct application of method.

(continued)

(continued)

	Level One	**Level Two**	**Level Three**	**Level Four**
Communication	Explanations are unclear and difficult to follow.	Explanations are coherent, but reveal imperfect understanding of the problem.	Explanations are clear and reflect understanding of most parts of the problem.	Explanations are clear and reflect understanding of all parts of the problem.

Middle School Mathematics Performance Tasks ◆ 85

BASKETBALL CAMP

Mathematics Assessed

- ◆ Number Operations and Concepts
- ◆ Problem Solving and mathematical Reasoning
- ◆ Mathematical Skills and Tools
- ◆ Mathematical Communication.

Directions to the Students

Kristin won a 7-day scholarship worth $1,000 to the Pro Shot Basketball Camp, but she will have to make some decisions about how to spend the money. Round trip travel expenses to the camp are $335 by air or $125 by train. At the camp she must choose between a week of individual instruction at $60 per day or a week of group instruction at $40 per day. Kristen's food and other living expenses are fixed at $45 per day. If she cannot add more money to the scholarship award, what are all the possible choices of travel and instruction plans that Kristen could afford to make?

Decide how you would recommend that Kristen spend her award, and write a brief letter to her explaining your thinking.

* This task is slightly adapted from one developed by the National Assessment of Educational Progress (NAEP) for its 1992 assessment.

About This Task

In this task, students must differentiate between fixed costs (living expenses) and variable expenses, and they must recognize that there are trade-offs to be made between different forms of travel and different forms of instruction. They must make accurate calculations and explain their thinking.

Solution

Kristin's fixed expenses will be $7 \times \$45$ or $315.00 for the 7 days, for food and living expenses. Therefore, she has $1,000 - \$315$ or $685 to spend for travel and instruction. The group plan will cost 7 × \$40 or \$280 for the week while the individual plan will cost 7 × \$60 or \$420 for the week. Therefore, Kristin has three options that she can afford with the available funds:

Group instruction and train travel:	\$280 + \$125 = \$405 with \$280 remaining
Group instruction and plane travel:	\$280 + \$335 = \$615 with \$70 remaining
Individual instruction and train travel:	\$420 + \$125 = \$545 with \$140 remaining

Kristin does not have enough money to pay for individual instruction and plane travel since that would come to \$420 + \$335 or \$755, \$70 more than the \$685 available after the fixed expenses are paid for. Individual recommendations will vary.

Rubric

	Level One	Level Two	Level Three	Level Four
Problem Solving Approach	The student doesn't use a method or the method used is completely inappropriate.	The student uses an appropriate method, but does not fully execute it.	The student uses an appropriate method.	The student uses a method that is elegant and efficient, revealing comprehensive understanding.
Accuracy and Procedural Skill	Major errors in calculation, resulting in erroneous conclusions.	Some computational errors, resulting in minor errors in conclusions.	Only minor computational errors; results are still correct.	No computational errors.
Communication	Explanation is muddled and difficult to follow.	Intent of the explanation is fairly clear, but not well executed.	Explanation is clear.	In addition, the explanation reveals understanding of trade-offs.

Middle School Mathematics Performance Tasks ◆ 87

BULL'S EYE

Mathematics Assessed

- ◆ Number Operations and Concepts
- ◆ Geometry and Measurement
- ◆ Functions and Algebra
- ◆ Statistics and Probability
- ◆ Problem Solving and Mathematical Reasoning
- ◆ Mathematical Skills and Tools
- ◆ Mathematical Communication.

Directions to the Student

The archery target shown below is made of four circles, with radii of 1 foot, 2 feet, 3 feet, and 4 feet, and with points as marked. If you shoot an arrow at random at the target, and it does not miss the target altogether, what is the probability that you will earn a score of 10? What is the probability of earning a 7? a 5? a 3?

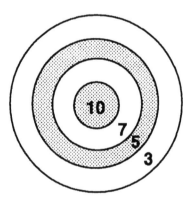

Write an explanation that a younger student could understand, describing how you arrived at your answers.

About This Task

In this task, students must apply concepts of geometry, proportions, and probability to calculate the probability of earning each score. They must find the areas of the different concentric circles, or at least their ratios, to determine the likelihood of a randomly-shot arrow landing in each of the rings.

Solution

Note: The solution that follows is based on the 3.14 approximation of pi. The area of a circle may be found by applying the formula a = π r². The area of the smallest circle is 3.14 square feet (3.14 × 1 × 1). The most efficient way to solve the first problem is to recognize that the area of a circle varies in proportion to the square of the radius, and since the area of the entire target is 3.14 × 4 × 4, the probability of hitting a bull's eye is one chance in 16. Through calculation, one can demonstrate that the area of the entire target is 3.14 × 4 × 4 = 50.24 square feet, and that

$$\frac{3.14}{50.24} = \frac{1}{16} \text{ or } 6.25\%$$

As for the other scores, students must find the areas of each of the rings of the target. Using this approach, the area of the bull's eye circle is 3.14. The area of the next ring is 9.42 square feet [(3.14 × 2 × 2) − 3.14]. The area of the third ring is 15.70 square feet [(3.14 × 3 × 3) − (3.14 × 2 × 2)] or (28.26 − 12.56). The area of the outside ring is 31.40 square feet [(3.14 × 4 × 4) − (3.14 × 3 × 3)] or (50.24 − 28.26).

Therefore the ratio of the area of the second circle to the total area of the target is:

$$\frac{9.42}{50.24} = \frac{1}{5.3} = 18.75\%$$

The ratio of the area of the third circle to the total area of the target is:

$$\frac{15.70}{50.24} = \frac{1}{3.2} = 31.25\%$$

The ratio of the area of the outside circle to the total area of the target is:

$$\frac{21.98}{50.24} = \frac{1}{2.3} = 43.75\%$$

The answers may be checked by adding the probabilities of each of the rings, and determining that the sum is 100% (6.25% + 18.75% + 31.25% + 43.75% = 100%).

There are many possibilities for error in this problem. Some students may believe that since the bull's eye circle has a radius of 1, while the largest circle has a radius of 4, that a randomly-shot arrow has one chance in four of hitting the center circle. Others may make errors in their calculations of the area of each of the rings, subtracting just the area of the next smaller ring, rather than the areas of all the previous rings.

Rubric

	Level One	Level Two	Level Three	Level Four
Problem Solving Approach	Approach to the problem is disorganized, with no systematic approach.	Approach reveals some attempt at organization, but not completely carried through.	Approach is organized, and if followed would yield a correct solution.	Approach used is highly organized and systematic, with evidence of careful planning.
Accuracy and Procedural Skill	Many errors in calculations, yielding wildly erroneous results.	Some computational inaccuracies, resulting in minor errors in the result.	Only minor errors in calculations; correct application of formulas.	No errors in computation; correct application of formulas and use of calculator.
Communication	Explanation unclear and difficult to follow.	Explanation is coherent, but reveals imperfect understanding of the problem.	Explanation is clear and reflects understanding of the problem.	Explanation is not only clear but is also well structured to illustrate the relationship between the different rings.

CHALK IT UP!

Mathematics Assessed

- ◆ Geometry and Measurement Concepts
- ◆ Number and Operations Concepts
- ◆ Problem Solving and Mathematical Reasoning
- ◆ Mathematical Skills and Tools
- ◆ Mathematical Communication
- ◆ Algebra Concepts.

Directions to the Student

In California, 5,678 school children set a record for the largest chalk pavement art. Their drawing was 90,000 square feet. It took 12 days to complete.

a. Assuming that the boundary of the drawing is a square, how long is a side? Show how you found your answer.
b. How many square feet were colored by each child if each child got to color the same area? Show how you found your answer.
c. If a piece of sidewalk chalk covers 25 square feet of pavement, how many pieces of chalk might have been used in making this drawing? Show how you found your answer.
d. The sketch below shows one of the first drawings of the pavement art. How many square feet do you think the lizard covers? Explain how you arrived at your answer.

About This Task

In this task, students approximate the area of an irregular shape, determine side length given area, and use proportional reasoning.

Solution

a. 300 feet since $s^2 = 90,000$, $s = \sqrt{90,000} = 300$
b. almost 16 square feet since $90,000 / 5,678 \approx 15.85$
c. 3,600 pieces since $90,000 / 25 = 3,600$
d. An approximation indicating that the lizard takes up between about 50,000 and 70,000 square feet with a clear and viable explanation of how students arrived at the approximation. For example, students may say that the area is about of 60,000 square feet because they used the grid to count up the lizard-free areas and the partially lizard free areas and got about 19 out of 56 grid squares which means that the lizard covers about 37 out of 56 grid squares. So, the area covered by the lizard would be about 66% or 2/3 of 90,000 which is about 60,000 square feet.

Rubric

	Level One	Level Two	Level Three	Level Four
Problem Solving Approach	Method used to find the area is disorganized, with no systematic method.	Method used to find the area reveals some attempt at consistency, but not completely carried through.	Method used to find the area is consistent, and if followed would yield correct solutions.	Method used to find the area is consistent and reveals recognition of the significance of the remainder.
Accuracy and Procedural Skill	Many errors in calculations, yielding wildly erroneous results.	Some computational inaccuracies, resulting in minor errors in the results.	Only minor errors in calculations; correct application of method.	No errors in computation; correct application of method.
Communication	Explanations and work are unclear and difficult to follow.	Explanations and work are coherent, but reveal imperfect understanding of the problem.	Explanations and work are clear and reflect understanding of most parts of the problem.	Explanations and work are clear and reflect understanding of all parts of the problem.

Middle School Mathematics Performance Tasks ◆ 93

CHECKERS TOURNAMENT

Mathematics Assessed

- ◆ Probability (combinations)
- ◆ Problem Solving and Mathematical Reasoning
- ◆ Mathematical Skills and Tools
- ◆ Mathematical Communication.

Directions to the Student

Josh, Mike, Stacy, and Carrie have decided to organize a checkers tournament, with themselves as players. If they each play each of the others once only, how many games will be played?

Describe in words the method you used to figure out your answer. You may want to organize your information in a table or make some other "picture" to represent the tournament.

As an extension, determine how many games would have to be played if a fifth student, and a sixth, were added to the tournament.

About This Task

This assessment task involves the number of different paired combinations of a small set of numbers. (This is somewhat different from a permutations problem, in that the game between Josh and Mike is the same as that between Mike and Josh.) The challenge for the student is to organize a method to identify all the possible combinations that is systematic and comprehensive. This is not difficult with a small number of competitors in the tournament, but only if the system is a good one will a student be able to extend it to a fifth and sixth competitor.

Solution

Since there are four competitors in the tournament, each individual must play each other person, or three others. This may be illustrated by enumerating all the possible combinations, as, for example:

94 ◆ Middle School Mathematics Performance Tasks

Josh – Mike

Josh – Stacy

Josh – Carrie

Mike – Stacy

Mike – Carrie

Stacy – Carrie

From this list, it is apparent that there are six games to be played. As other competitors are added, the list becomes correspondingly longer.

A more efficient method is to reason that since each individual must play a game with each other individual, the number of games to be played is 4×3 or 12. However, since this method counts permutations rather than combinations (that is, it counts the game between Mike and Josh twice—as Mike–Josh and Josh–Mike), it yields an answer that is double the correct answer. Therefore, the correct answer is $12 \div 2$ or 6.

Hence, if another player is added, the number of games is $5 \times 4 = 20 \div 2 = 10$. For six players, the number of games is $6 \times 5 = 30 \div 2 = 15$.

Rubric

	Level One	Level Two	Level Three	Level Four
Problem Solving Approach	The student doesn't use a method or the method used is completely inappropriate.	The student uses an appropriate method, but does not fully execute it.	The student uses an appropriate method.	The student uses a method that is elegant and efficient, revealing comprehensive understanding.
Communication	Explanation is not provided or is unclear. Information randomly presented.	Explanation reveals the intention of a systematic approach, but is not completely clear. Some attempt to organize the information; however the system is ineffective.	Explanation clearly describes a systematic approach. Adequate organization of information in table or tree graph form.	Explanation is systematic and makes explicit recognition of a pattern. In addition, the organization of information is highly systematic and neatly presented.

Middle School Mathematics Performance Tasks ◆ 95

Samples of Student Work

This problem presents an interesting challenge for students, and permits many possible ways to organize the information. Most students are able to find an approach to the problem, but very few are able to discern the generalized pattern, or make a systematic extension to more players in the tournament.

Level One

		Josh	Mike	Stacy	Carrie	Ken
Josh			✓	✓	✓	✓
Mike		✓		✓	✓	✓
Stacy		✓	✓		✓	✓
Carrie		✓	✓	✓		✓
Ken		✓	✓	✓	✓	

> To figure out this problem I put the names on the tops and side of the paper. I put lines through the paper to make twenty-five boxes. When I put check in the boxes it meant that Josh, Mike, Stacy, Carrie, and Ken set ups someone elses set of checkers. As you read on this chart I came up with twenty check

This response organizes the information in a rudimentary manner. However, the student fails to recognize that given this approach, each student would play every other student twice. Furthermore, the response gives no actual answer to the question.

96 ◆ Middle School Mathematics Performance Tasks

Level Two

Josh	Mike	Stacy	Carrie	Ken
Mike	Stacy	Carrie	Ken	
Stacy	Carrie	Ken		
Carrie	Ken			
Ken				

What I did was I made a chart and put the five names on the side. Then I matched up all the names together. I also made sure that the children only played each other once. So, Josh played first, he played Mike, then he played Stacy, then Carrie, and last, but not least he played Ken. Now it is Mike's turn. Mike first plays Stacy, then played Carrie, and last played Ken. Mike does not play Josh again. It's Stacy's turn. First she played Carrie, then she played Ken. But, Stacy doesn't play Josh or Mike again. Now it is Carrie's turn. She can only play Ken. She can not play Stacy, Mike, & Josh. Now it is Ken's turn, but he can't play anyone, because he has already played them all. That is how I organized my chart.

This response organizes the information adequately, but gives no answer to the question. Furthermore, the student appears to confuse the sequence of organizing the information with the sequence of play in a tournament.

Level Two

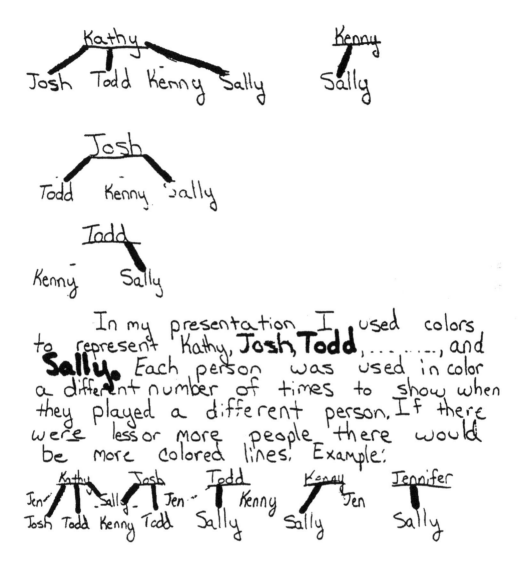

This response provides no answer to the question and the explanation is difficult to follow. However, the student appears to understand the situation and the organization would be adequate to solve the problem.

98 ◆ Middle School Mathematics Performance Tasks

Level Three

I solved this problem by drawing a line from one name to the name below it. When I counted all of the lines to the names I got ten. Josh equaled four, Mike equaled three, Stacy equaled two, Carrie equaled one, and Ken equaled zero.

This response is rated a Level Three minus. It accurately organizes the information and provides an explanation that is fairly clear.

Middle School Mathematics Performance Tasks ◆ 99

Level Three

How I organized my chart is that I put the word "Play" so that the person that might read this would know who played who. I also put the words "Already Pl. so that the person would know that that person already played the other people or person.

Answer: 10 plays

Josh	Mike	Stacy	Carrie	Kenny
Play	Play	Play	Play	Already P
1. Josh, Mike	5. Mike, Stacy	8. Stacy, Carrie	10. Carrie, Kenny	Carrie
			Already Pl.	Stacy
2. Josh, Stacy	6. Mike, Carrie	9. Stacy, Kenny	Stacy	Mike
		Already Pl.	Mike	Josh
3. Josh, Carrie	7. Mike, Kenny	Mike	Josh	
	Already Pl.	Josh		
4. Josh, Kenny	Josh			

This response provides the correct answer to the question using a well-organized approach. The explanation is clear.

Level Four

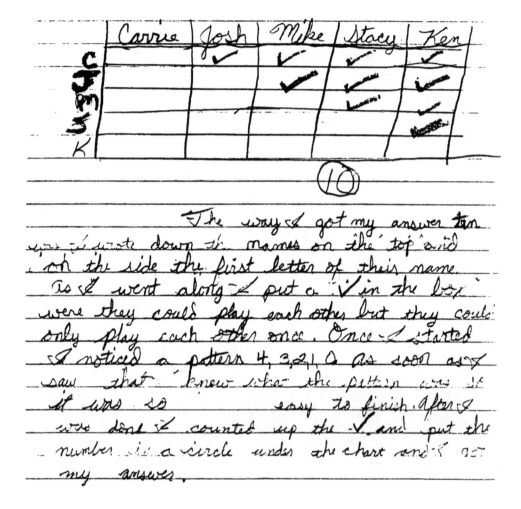

The way I got my answer ten was I wrote down the names on the top and on the side the first letter of their name. As I went along I put a ✓ in the box were they could play each other but they could only play each other once. Once I started I noticed a pattern 4, 3, 2, 1, 0. As soon as I saw that I knew what the pattern was & it was so easy to finish. After I was done I counted up the ✓ and put the number in a circle under the chart and I got my answer.

This response is rated a Level Four. The information is clear and the response makes explicit recognition that the situation can be efficiently solved through applying a pattern.

Middle School Mathematics Performance Tasks ◆ 101

Level Four

Josh	Kathy	Todd	Kenny	Sally
Josh, Kathy	Kathy, Todd	Todd, Kenny	Kenny, Sally	Sally was
Josh, Todd	Kathy, Kenny	Todd, Sally		mentioned
Josh, Kenny	Kathy, Sally			three tim
Josh, Sally				before +
				has no
				one to
				play.

$$4 + 3 = 7 + 2 = 9 + 1 = 10$$

10 games will be played

The way I figuerd this out was I made a chart having each player play another player 1 time. When I was finished doing that I added up and got my answer of 10.

extended

Josh	Kathy	Todd	Kenny	Sally	Mar_
Josh, Kathy	Kathy, Todd	Todd, Ken	Ken, Sally	Sally Mary	Agair
Josh, Todd	Kathy, Kenny	Told, Sally	Ken, Mary		mary
Josh, Ken	Kath, Sally	Todd, mary			was
Josh, Sally	Kathy, Mary				play=
Josh, Mary					befc.

$$\_ 15 \text{ games} \quad 5 + 4 = 9 + 3 = 12 + 2 + 1 = 15 \qquad 64$$

This response is rated a Level Four minus because, while it provides a correct answer to the basic question and to the extension, it makes no explicit recognition of a pattern in the information.

102 ◆ Middle School Mathematics Performance Tasks

COUNTRY MILE

Mathematics Assessed

- ◆ Number Operations and Concepts
- ◆ Geometry and Measurement
- ◆ Functions and Algebra
- ◆ Problem Solving and Mathematical Reasoning
- ◆ Mathematical Skills and Tools
- ◆ Mathematical Communication.

Directions to the Student

In an old folk tale, a poor peasant is offered as much land as he can walk around from sunup to sundown. If you were given that offer, how much land could you claim? What shape would it be?

In order to answer these questions, you may want to:

- ◆ Determine the length of a day from sunup to sundown. Is it the same every day? If not, at which time of year would you choose to make your walk?
- ◆ Determine how fast you can walk in an hour, and how many hours you could walk in the day. You should consider the need for food and rest during the day.
- ◆ Determine the best shape to walk around to claim the most land. Will it be a square? Some other rectangle? A circle? Some other shape?
- ◆ Calculate the amount of land (in square miles) that you could claim.

Your answer should include:

- ◆ Drawings of the different possible shapes you might use, with their respective areas and perimeters.
- ◆ A clear presentation of the methods you used to calculate:

  - the length of the day
  - the distance you can walk
  - the area you can claim.

- ◆ All work should be clearly labeled.

About This Task

This task involves the relationship between area and perimeter, and the fact that for a given perimeter, the largest enclosed area is a circle. Of the rectangular shapes, a square encloses more area than a rectangle. Students will have to know that the longest day of the year is at the summer solstice and they will have to

- ◆ determine how fast s/he can walk in an hour, possibly by measuring the distance that can be walked in 15 minutes, and extending that to an hour,
- ◆ estimate the amount of time needed for meals, rests, etc.,
- ◆ calculate the distance that can be walked in a day and the area enclosed,
- ◆ make clear drawings of the different possible shapes, and
- ◆ write a clear description of the process used.

As written, this task presents extensive "scaffolding" through the bulleted list of steps to be used in solving it. It could be given to students without those hints, making it correspondingly more difficult. Additionally, the algebraic formula, $d = rt$, can be used in solving the problem.

Solution

Answers will vary, depending on the assumptions made, but here is one possibility:

At the summer solstice, it is light from approximately 5 a.m. to 9 p.m., an elapsed time of 16 hours. A person would need to rest for about 2 hours in that time, leaving 14 hours for walking (assuming a high level of physical fitness). If one were able to walk on roads, one could walk about 3 miles per hour, or 42 miles in the course of the 14 hours. If one had to walk across fields, the rate would be more like 2 miles per hour at most, or 28 miles during the 14 hours.

If one walked on roads, the most efficient shape might be a square, with a side of 10.5 miles, and an area of 110 square miles. If one walked through fields, and could make a circle, the rate of 2 miles per hour would allow for a circumference of 28 miles, a diameter of 8.9 miles, a radius of 4.5 miles, and an area of 63.7 square miles. If, on the other hand, it were possible to maintain the same 3 miles per hour rate walking across fields, and one could walk 42 miles in a circle, the enclosed area would have a circumference

104 ◆ Middle School Mathematics Performance Tasks

of 42 miles, a diameter of 13.4 miles, a radius of 6.7 miles, and an area of 141 square miles. Hence, the rate one can walk is the most important factor affecting the amount of area that could be claimed.

Rubric

	Level One	Level Two	Level Three	Level Four
Problem Solving Approach	The student doesn't use a method or the method used is completely inappropriate.	The student uses an appropriate method, but does not fully execute it.	The student uses an appropriate method.	The student uses a method that is elegant and efficient, revealing comprehensive understanding.
Accuracy and Procedural Skill	Solution is unsupported.	Solution is accurate but the computations do not fully support the solution.	Solution is accurate, with minor computational errors	Solution is accurate, and the calculations demonstrate understanding of the structure of the problem.
Communication	No drawings are provided or no determination of relative areas for shapes of the same perimeter.	Drawings of shapes reveal an attempt to analyze different shapes but they include substantive errors.	Drawings of shapes indicate analysis of area and perimeter but there are minor errors in the execution.	Drawings of shapes indicate careful analysis of shapes and their areas and perimeters.

Middle School Mathematics Performance Tasks ◆ 105

EENY, MEENY, MINY, MOE

Mathematics Assessed

- ◆ Number and Operations Concepts
- ◆ Problem Solving and Mathematical Reasoning
- ◆ Mathematical Skills and Tools
- ◆ Mathematical Communication.

Directions to the Student

Eeny, meeny, miny, moe,
Catch a tiger by the toe.
If he hollers, let him go,
Eeny, meeny, miny, moe.
My mother told me
To pick the very best one
And you are it!

Children around the world use the counting rhyme Eeny, Meeny, Miny, Moe to select someone to be counted out in a game. One child, the chanter, points from person to person and then points to himself with each syllable, continuing until someone is out. The person who is pointed to on the last syllable, "it," is counted out.

a. How many syllables are in the version of the counting rhyme given above?
b. Indicate if the chanter would be counted out for each number of players given below.

  (1) Two children.
  (2) Three children.
  (3) Four children.
  (4) Five children.
  (5) Six children.

c. How does the number of syllables and the number of players affect whether or not the chanter will be counted out?
d. Suppose that there are 108 syllables in a rhyme that is played like Eeny, Meeny, Miny, Moe and that there are nine players, will the chanter be counted out? What is an easy way to figure that out?

106 ◆ Middle School Mathematics Performance Tasks

e.

    (1) Suppose a truck leaves New York City on a Sunday and arrives in Los Angeles 10 days later, on which day of the week did the truck arrive in Los Angeles?

    (2) Give the lengths of five trips of different durations that would result in the truck arriving in Los Angeles on that same day of the week, assuming the trips all start on a Sunday? What is an easy way to figure that out?

f.   What does the Eeny, Meeny, Miny, Moe problem have in common with the truck problem?

g.   What other kinds of problems might be solved in the same way as the Eeny, Meeny, Miny, Moe problem and the truck problem?

About This Task

In this task, students realize that a remainder may be much more than just a leftover to be ignored but it can play a significant role in analyzing patterns, communicating relationships, and problem solving. Additionally, the task can serve as an introduction to or as a reinforcement of modular arithmetic.

Solution

a.   44 since by line the syllable count is:

Ee/ny, mee/ny, mi/ny, moe, (7)
Catch a ti/ger by the toe. (7)
If he hol/lers, let him go, (7)
Ee/ny, mee/ny, mi/ny, moe. (7)
My moth/er told me (5)
To pick the ver/y best one (7)
And you are it! (4)

b.   Note: consider the chanter as person 0 and the first person pointed to as person 1 and so on.

    (1) Yes, 44/2 yields a remainder of 0 so the chanter is out.

    (2) No, 44/3 yields a remainder of 2 so the second person pointed to is out.

    (3) Yes, 44/4 yields a remainder of 0 so the chanter is out.

Middle School Mathematics Performance Tasks ◆ 107

      (4) No, 44/5 yields a remainder of 4 so the fourth person pointed to is out.

      (5) No, 44/6 yields a remainder of 2 so the second person pointed to is out.

c. The chanter will be counted out if the remainder is zero when the number of syllables is divided by the number of players.

d. Yes, chanter will be counted out. Divide 108 by 9 and see if the remainder is 0.

e.

      (1) The truck would arrive in Los Angeles on a Wednesday since 10/7 yields a remainder of 3. (Note: This works if we consider Sunday as day 0 just like the counter in Eeny, Meeny, Miny, Moe is counted as 0.)

      (2) A 3 day trip, a 10 day trip, a 17 day trip, a 24 day trip, and a 31 day trip would also arrive on a Wednesday since each of those numbers divided by 7 yields a remainder of 3. An easy way to figure it out is to take multiples of 7 and add 3.

f. They are both about remainders and multiples. In the Eeny, Meeny, Miny, Moe problem the chanter is out when the number of syllables is a multiple of the number of players—that is, the remainder is zero when the number of syllables is divided by the number of players. In the truck problem, the truck arrives on Wednesday when the number of days is 3 more than a multiple of 7—that is, the remainder is three when number of days is divided by 7.

g. Anything that involves modular arithmetic could work such as determining what time it will be x number of hours from now.

Rubric

	Level One	Level Two	Level Three	Level Four
Problem Solving Approach	Method used to solve the problem is disorganized, with no systematic method.	Method reveals some attempt at consistency, but not completely carried through.	Method is consistent, and if followed would yield correct solutions.	Method is consistent and reveals recognition of the significance of the remainder.

(continued)

(continued)

	Level One	Level Two	Level Three	Level Four
Accuracy and Procedural Skill	Many errors in calculations, yielding wildly erroneous results.	Some computational inaccuracies, resulting in minor errors in the results.	Only minor errors in calculations; correct application of method.	No errors in computation; correct application of method.
Communication	Explanations are unclear and difficult to follow.	Explanations are coherent, but reveal imperfect understanding of the problem.	Explanations are clear and reflect understanding of most parts of the problem.	Explanations are clear and reflect understanding of all parts of the problem.

HOLLYWOOD STARS

Mathematics Assessed

- Geometry and Measurement Concepts
- Number and Operations Concepts
- Problem Solving and Mathematical Reasoning
- Mathematical Skills and Tools
- Mathematical Communication.

Directions to the Student

Pixar Animation Studios uses transformational geometry to animate the shapes and images created by their artists for movies like *Inside Out*, *Brave*, and *Toy Story*. (You can watch a video about it at http://ed.ted.com/lessons/pixar-the-math-behind-the-movies-tony-derose.)

a. Suppose that you work for Pixar and are to design a program that will move a star across the sky. In particular, your program must move the four pointed star at position A to B then to C then to D then to E finally ending in the enlarged star at position F.

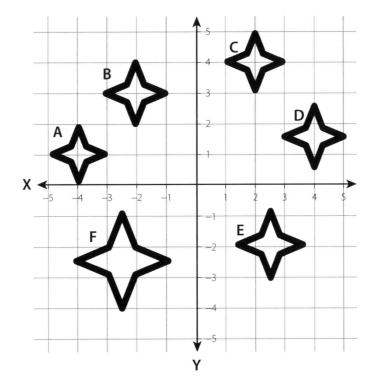

Give the details, in order, of each transformation that you would use to make the star move across the sky and increase in size as described above.

b. Suppose that after the stars are moved across the sky, the star at position F is translated right 2.5 units and up 2.5 units, dilated by a scale factor of 2 about the origin, and then rotated 810 degrees clockwise about the origin. Sketch its final image on the grid below.

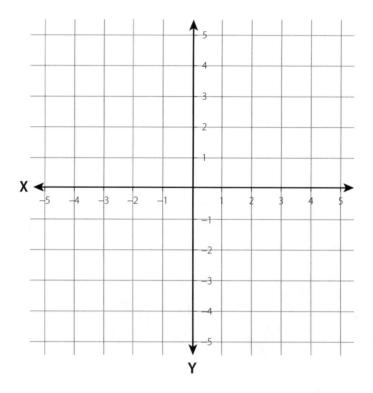

c. Pixar uses a command called subdivide to create a smooth curve from a polygon by finding the midpoints of the sides and then moving those midpoints to the midpoints of their clockwise neighbors; that is, to the clockwise adjacent line segment. For example, as shown in the following sequence, if you start with a quadrilateral, you would first find the midpoints of its sides and then move those midpoints to their clockwise neighbors. Once a smooth curve has been created, it can be animated by moving any of the original vertices.

Middle School Mathematics Performance Tasks ♦ 111

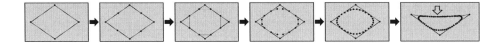

(1) Find the coordinates of the first set of midpoints: A, B, C, and D.

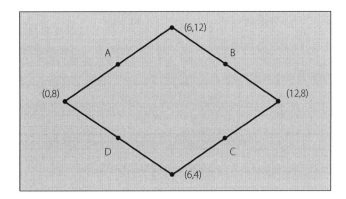

(2) Find the coordinates of the second set of midpoints (the clockwise neighbors of the first set of midpoints): E, F, G, H, I, J, K, and L.

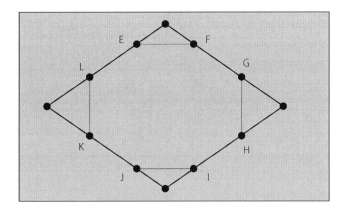

d. If you were an artist for Pixar what kind of character might you create and what kinds of transformations might you use to animate it?

About This Task

In the first part of this task, students perform plane transformations in the way that is done in film animations. In the second part of the task, they find midpoints to illustrate another engaging application of coordinate geometry. Showing students the video at http://ed.ted.com/lessons/pixar-the-math-behind-the-movies-tony-derose is a good way to set the stage for this task.

Solution

a. To move

- A to B, translate 2 units right and 2 units up.
- B to C, translate 4 units right and 1 unit up.
- C to D, translate 2 units right and 2.5 units down.
- D to E, translate 1.5 units left and 3.5 units down.
- E to F, translate 5 units left and 0.5 units down.

To increase the size of the star at Position F, dilate about its center by a scale factor of 1.5.

b.

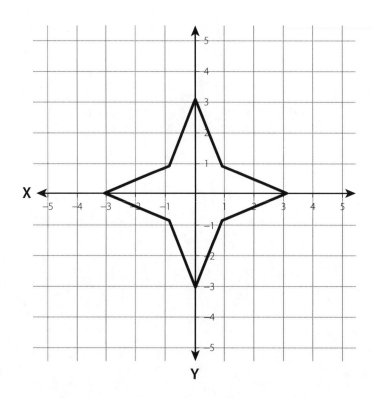

c.

(1) A (3,10), B (9,10), C (9,6), D (3,6);
(3) E (4.5,11), F (7.5,11), G (10.5, 9), H (10.5, 7), I (7.5, 5), J (4.5, 5),
     K (1.5,7), L (1.5, 9).

d. Many possible responses.

Rubric

	Level One	Level Two	Level Three	Level Four
Problem Solving Approach	Method used to determine images and transformation is disorganized, with no systematic method.	Method used to determine images and transformation reveals some attempt at consistency, but not completely carried through.	Method used to determine images and transformation is consistent, and if followed would yield correct solutions.	Method used to determine images and transformation is consistent.
Accuracy and Procedural Skill	Many errors in calculations, yielding wildly erroneous results.	Some computational inaccuracies, resulting in minor errors in the results.	Only minor errors in calculations; correct application of method.	No errors in computation; correct application of method.
Communication	Graph of resulting images is missing or not similar to the pre-image.

Description of what student would animate is given but transformations are too vague or would most likely not result in the character. | Graph of resulting images is erred with respect to two transformations.

Description of what student would animate is given but it is unclear if the transformations stated would result in the character. | Graph of resulting images is erred with respect to one transformation.

Description of what student would animate and the transformations used are clearly stated and would result in most features the character chosen. | Graph of resulting images is correct.

Description of what student would animate and the transformations used are clearly stated and likely would be used to animate the character chosen. |

114 ◆ Middle School Mathematics Performance Tasks

LINEUP

Mathematics Assessed

- ◆ Number Operations and Concepts
- ◆ Functions and Algebra
- ◆ Statistics and Probability
- ◆ Problem Solving and Mathematical Reasoning
- ◆ Mathematical Skills and Tools
- ◆ Mathematical Communication.

Directions to the Student

A baseball team has nine players; the order in which they bat is called the "batting order" or "lineup." How many different lineups are possible? Write a brief description explaining your reasoning to the coach of your school's baseball team.

About This Task

This task requires students to apply the concept of permutations to a practical situation. It may be used to introduce students to the concept of factorials.

Solution

In a team with nine members, there are 362,880 possible lineups, a surprisingly high number. In order to solve the problem successfully, students will probably have to use a calculator; it should certainly be available to them. Students may approach the problem in several different ways; some possibilities are presented below:

- ◆ Students may analyze the number of possible lineups in a team with only 3 members, then 4, then 5, and discern the pattern. They may list these possibilities, or make them into a chart of some kind.
- ◆ Students may reason that any of the 9 members could bat in the first position, followed by any of the remaining 8 in the second position, any of the remaining 7 in the third position, and so forth.

An error that some students may make is to add rather than multiply which would result in an answer of 45 ($9 + 8 + 7 + 6 + 5 + 4 + 3 + 2 + 1$) rather than 362,880 ($9 \times 8 \times 7 \times 6 \times 5 \times 4 \times 3 \times 2 \times 1$).

Rubric

	Level One	Level Two	Level Three	Level Four
Problem Solving Approach	The student doesn't use a method or the method used is completely inappropriate.	The student uses an appropriate method, but does not fully execute it.	The student uses an appropriate method.	The student uses a method that is elegant and efficient, revealing comprehensive understanding.
Accuracy and Procedural Skill	Solution is unsupported.	Solution is accurate but the computations do not fully support the solution.	Solution is accurate, with minor computational errors.	Solution is accurate, and the calculations demonstrate understanding of the structure of the problem.
Communication	Description is completely missing or inadequate. The student randomly presents information.	Description conveys some aspects of the method the student used for solving the problem, but is incomplete. The student attempts to organize the information; however it is incomplete or leads to errors.	Description adequately conveys a systematic method for solving the problem. The student organizes information in a fairly systematic manner.	Description clearly conveys an elegant and efficient method for solving the problem. In addition, the explanation reveals an understanding of the patterns inherent in the situation, e.g., how to solve similar problems. The student organizes information in an efficient and systematic manner.

116 ◆ Middle School Mathematics Performance Tasks

LOCKER COMBINATIONS

Mathematics Assessed

- ◆ Number Operations and Concepts
- ◆ Functions and Algebra
- ◆ Statistics and Probability
- ◆ Problem Solving and Mathematical Reasoning
- ◆ Mathematical Skills and Tools
- ◆ Mathematical Communication.

Directions to the Student

Many school locker combination locks have 30 numbers on their dials, and a series of three numbers (right, left, right) opens the lock. If you forgot your combination, and decided to try all the possible combinations, how many would you have to try? How long do you think it might take you if your combination were the last of all possible combinations that you tried?

Write a brief explanation for your school newspaper explaining how safe you believe combination locks to be.

About This Task

In this task, students must apply the concept of permutations to a practical situation, and then integrate those findings with estimates regarding time.

Solution

Answers will vary to some extent, depending on the assumptions made about time. But all answers should include reasoning such as the following:

- ◆ Since there are 30 numbers on the lock, and a series of three numbers makes up a combination, there are approximately $30 \times 29 \times 29$ possible combinations, or 25,230. (The reason for the "29" rather than "30" in the expression is because a combination would not contain two identical numbers next to one another, such as 5-5-28. Some students may offer other such refinements.) If the school's locks have more or fewer numbers, the answers will be correspondingly different.

- ◆ In order to test all the possible combinations, one would need a systematic approach, so one could be sure of which ones had been tested. This would take some time to devise.
- ◆ It is possible to try a combination in about 15 seconds. Therefore, to test 25,230 combinations would require 6,307 minutes, or about 105 hours. Since this is a considerable amount of time, it is likely that combination locks offer a fairly secure protection of students' belongings.

Rubric

	Level One	Level Two	Level Three	Level Four
Problem Solving Approach	The student doesn't use a method or the method used is completely inappropriate.	The student uses an appropriate method, but does not fully execute it.	The student uses an appropriate method.	The student uses a method that is elegant and efficient, revealing comprehensive understanding.
Accuracy and Procedural Skill	Solution is unsupported.	Solution is accurate but the computations do not fully support the solution.	Solution is accurate, with minor computational errors.	Solution is accurate, and the calculations demonstrate understanding of the structure of the problem.
Communication	Description is completely missing or inadequate. The student randomly presents information.	Description conveys some aspects of the method the student used for solving the problem, but is incomplete. The student attempts to organize the information; however it is incomplete or leads to errors.	Description adequately conveys a systematic method for solving the problem. The student organizes information in a fairly systematic manner.	Description clearly conveys an elegant and efficient method for solving the problem. In addition, the explanation reveals an understanding of the patterns inherent in the situation, e.g., how to solve similar problems. The student organizes information in an efficient and systematic manner.

118 ◆ Middle School Mathematics Performance Tasks

LUCKY SODA

Mathematics Assessed

- ◆ Number Operations and Concepts
- ◆ Functions and Algebra
- ◆ Statistics and Probability
- ◆ Problem Solving and Mathematical Reasoning
- ◆ Mathematical Skills and Tools
- ◆ Mathematical Communication.

Directions to the Students

A soft drink company has hired you to help organize a promotion for its Cool Mist soft drink by including prizes in some of the bottles. The prizes will be tokens attached to the insides of the lids of the bottles; customers determine whether they have won by scratching the lids.

The soft drink company has created two types of prizes: "gold" awards and "silver" awards; the gold awards are $10.00 coupons for Cool Mist and the silver awards are $2.00 coupons. The company will put the prizes in 500 cases (12 bottles to a case) of soft drinks, but it needs a system to decide which bottles to put the winning lids on. They plan to award 25 gold prizes and 250 silver prizes, and they need a fair system for distributing them among all the bottles.

On the assembly line in the bottling plant, each bottle is assigned a number. Which bottles should be designated "gold" winners and which ones "silver" winners so the winning bottles are distributed through the entire 500 cases, and will therefore be distributed around the country? You should be sure that no bottle is assigned more than one prize.

To complete your job for the soft drink company, you should devise a method for awarding the gold and silver prizes such that:

- ◆ 25 gold prizes and 250 silver prizes are awarded
- ◆ no bottle has more than one prize
- ◆ the prizes are distributed evenly throughout the entire 500 cases.

Write a brief letter to the president of the soft drink company, explaining which bottles should have the gold and silver prizes, and the method you used to determine the winning bottles.

About This Task

This task requires that students calculate the total number of bottles of soft drink to be produced, and then to distribute the 275 prizes evenly among them. It primarily involves simple calculations, but a sequence for the calculations must be determined, and a system devised to ensure that no bottle is awarded more than one prize.

Solution

Several approaches are possible for this problem, although they all start with determining the number of bottles of soda in 500 cases ($500 \times 12 = 6{,}000$), and numbering the bottles from 1 to 6,000. One possible approach follows.

Step A: $6{,}000 \div 250 = 24$. Therefore, the silver prizes could be placed in one soda bottle of every 24, distributed throughout the 6,000, for example, in bottles numbered: 24, 48, 72, 96, etc.

Step B: $6{,}000 \div 25 = 240$. Therefore, the gold prizes could be placed in one soda bottle of every 240, distributed throughout the 6,000, for example, in bottles numbered: 240, 480, 720, 960, etc.

Step C: Since the bottles chosen for the gold prizes would have numbers that are divisible by 24, those silver prizes would have to be put in other bottles. Since there are 25 of those bottles, those silver prizes could be distributed throughout the 6,000 bottles, possibly in the bottles immediately prior to the gold prizes.

An alternate approach would be to proceed from the fact that there are 275 prizes altogether (250 silver and 25 gold). The prizes could be placed in every 21st bottle, with 10 silver followed by one gold, this pattern repeated 25 times.

120 ◆ Middle School Mathematics Performance Tasks

Rubric

	Level One	Level Two	Level Three	Level Four
Problem Solving Approach	The student doesn't use a method or the method used is completely inappropriate.	The student uses an appropriate method, but does not fully execute it.	The student uses an appropriate method.	The student uses a method that is elegant and efficient, revealing comprehensive understanding.
Accuracy and Procedural Skill	Solution is unsupported.	Solution is accurate but the computations do not fully support the solution.	Solution is accurate, with minor computational errors.	Solution is accurate, and the calculations demonstrate understanding of the structure of the problem.
Communication	Description is completely missing or inadequate. The student randomly presents information.	Description conveys some aspects of the method the student used for solving the problem, but is incomplete. The student attempts to organize the information; however it is incomplete or leads to errors.	Description adequately conveys a systematic method for solving the problem. The student organizes information in a fairly systematic manner.	Description clearly conveys an elegant and efficient method for solving the problem. In addition, the explanation reveals an understanding of the patterns inherent in the situation, e.g., how to solve similar problems. The student organizes information in an efficient and systematic manner.

Middle School Mathematics Performance Tasks ◆ 121

LUNCH MENU

Mathematics Assessed

- ◆ Statistics and Probability Concepts
- ◆ Number and Operations Concepts
- ◆ Problem Solving and Mathematical Reasoning
- ◆ Mathematical Skills and Tools
- ◆ Mathematical Communication.

Directions to the Student

A cafeteria that serves a district's middle school and high school is going to add a new item to their menu. Yi, a middle school student, and Ajay, a high school student, surveyed students at their schools to determine which of four possible new items being considered by the cafeteria students prefer. The number of middle school and high school students who voted for each option is given in the table below.

Possible New Menu Item	Number of Middle School Students	High School Students
Chicken quesadillas	12	14
Veggie burgers	9	14
Cheese ravioli	16	9
Turkey panini	13	13

- a. What percent of the high school students surveyed chose chicken quesadillas? Show how you found your answer.
- b. If the total high school enrollment is 800, how many of those students would you expect to prefer chicken quesadillas based on the survey results? Show how you found your answer.
- c. If the total middle school enrollment is 1,000, how many of those students would you expect to prefer chicken quesadillas based on the survey results? Show how you found your answer.

122 ◆ Middle School Mathematics Performance Tasks

d. Yi concludes that, based on the survey, we can say that the same number of high school as middle school students would like turkey paninis to be added to the menu. Ajay told Yi that her conclusion is wrong. Who is correct? Explain.

e. Based on the survey, which item would you recommend the cafeteria add to their menu? Explain including any assumptions that you make or anything else you think the cafeteria might consider in making their decision.

About This Task

In this task, students analyze the results of a survey and use that analysis to make a recommendation to the school cafeteria.

Solution

a. 28% since 50 students were surveyed and 14 preferred quesadillas; 14/50=28%.

b. 224 students since $0.28 \times 800 = 224$.

c. 240 students since 50 middle school students were surveyed and 12 chose quesadillas which is 24% and $0.24 \times 1,000 = 240$.

d. Yi is wrong since even though the same number of students surveyed preferred the paninis, that number does not represent the same number of students in each school.
26 percent of middle school students is 260 students but 26 percent of high school students is 208 students.

e. Based on the survey results, 464 students in total prefer chicken quesadillas, 404 prefer veggie burgers, 464 prefer ravioli, and 468 prefer paninis. So, most students may recommend adding paninis to the menu though it would be reasonable to suggest that adding any of the items under consideration except for the veggie burgers would be a good addition since the numbers are so close and surveys can be imperfect.

Assumptions: those surveyed are a representative sample of students, and those surveyed buy their lunch.

Rubric

	Level One	Level Two	Level Three	Level Four
Problem Solving Approach	Method used to analyze survey is disorganized, with no evidence of understanding how to interpret and apply results.	Method used to analyze survey shows limited understanding how to interpret and apply results.	Method used to analyze survey shows some understanding of how to interpret and apply results.	Method used to analyze survey shows clear understanding of how to interpret and apply results.
Accuracy and Procedural Skill	Many errors in calculations, yielding wildly erroneous results.	Some computational inaccuracies, resulting in minor errors in the results.	Only minor errors in calculations; correct application of method.	No errors in computation; correct application of method.
Communication	Explanations and work are unclear and difficult to follow.	Explanations and work are coherent, but reveal imperfect understanding of the problem.	Explanations and work are clear and reflect understanding of most parts of the problem.	Explanations and work are clear and reflect understanding of all parts of the problem.

124 ◆ Middle School Mathematics Performance Tasks

MONEY FROM TRASH

Mathematics Assessed

- ◆ Number Operations and Concepts
- ◆ Geometry and Measurement
- ◆ Functions and Algebra
- ◆ Problem Solving and Mathematical Reasoning
- ◆ Mathematical Skills and Tools
- ◆ Mathematical Communication.

Directions to the Student

The eighth grade students at Washington Middle School are trying to raise money to help pay for a class trip. There are 250 students in the class, and they want to raise $2,000.00 by recycling newspapers, cans, and glass and plastic bottles. Using the table below, calculate how many pounds of newspaper, cans, and bottles (or different combinations of these) students will have to collect to raise the money.

To complete this task:

- ◆ Determine how much each student is responsible to raise, and several ways students could fulfill their responsibilities.
- ◆ Based on the amount of newspaper, cans, and bottles your own family uses, decide which material you would collect for your contribution.
- ◆ Describe in words how you arrived at your conclusions.

Material	Amount per Ton
Mixed paper	$40 per ton
Newspaper	$100 per ton
Aluminum cans	$1,240 per ton
Steel cans	$50 per ton
Clear glass	$30 per ton

Amber glass	$15 per ton
Plastic soda bottles	$240 per ton
Plastic milk bottles	$300 per ton

About This Task

This task requires that students retrieve information from a table, make calculations using information from the table, collect information from their families, draw conclusions from information, and explain their reasoning in writing.

Solution

With 250 students in the class, and $2,000 to raise, each student must raise $8. According to the table, that $8 could be raised by recycling, for example, 160 lb. of newspaper, 13 lb. of aluminum cans, or 533 lb. of clear glass. Or, a student could raise the $8 through a combination of the different materials. Alternatively, students might elect to find another source of aluminum cans or newspapers, such as a Boys and Girls Club, or scout troop.

A complete table, showing the amount of each material worth $8.00, is presented on the next page:

Material	Amount per Ton	% Ton Worth $8.00	Number of Pounds Needed for $8.00
Mixed paper	$40	.20	400
Newspaper	$100	.08	160
Aluminum cans	$1240	.006	13
Steel cans	$50	.16	320
Clear glass	$30	.26	533
Amber glass	$15	.53	1067
Plastic soda bottles	$240	.03	67
Plastic milk bottles	$300	.026	53

Students will have to determine at least some of these calculations themselves, and incorporate them into their answer.

Students' narrative should show accurate reading of the original table, reasonable findings from the survey of home consumption, and should display awareness of the possible trade-offs involved. For example, a 32-ounce empty, glass juice bottle weighs approximately 12 oz. If a student were to try to raise his or her share of the money by recycling only juice bottles, 710 of them would be needed. Students can research possible tradeoffs by weighing recyclables or by searching the internet for information on the weights of recyclables

Rubric

	Level One	Level Two	Level Three	Level Four
Problem Solving Approach	The student doesn't use a method or the method used is completely inappropriate.	The student uses an appropriate method, but does not fully execute it.	The student uses an appropriate method.	The student uses a method that is elegant and efficient, revealing comprehensive understanding.
Accuracy and Procedural Skill	Solution is unsupported.	Solution is accurate but the computations do not fully support the solution.	Solution is accurate, with minor computational errors.	Solution is accurate, and the calculations demonstrate understanding of the structure of the problem.
Communication	Description is completely missing or inadequate. The student randomly presents information.	Description conveys some aspects of the method the student used for solving the problem, but is incomplete. The student attempts to organize the information; however it is incomplete or leads to errors.	Description adequately conveys a systematic method for solving the problem. The student organizes information in a fairly systematic manner.	Description clearly conveys an elegant and efficient method for solving the problem. In addition, the explanation reveals an understanding of the patterns inherent in the situation, e.g., how to solve similar problems. The student organizes information in an efficient and systematic manner.

Middle School Mathematics Performance Tasks ◆ 127

OUTFITS

Mathematics Assessed

- ◆ Number Operations and Concepts
- ◆ Functions and Algebra
- ◆ Statistics and Probability
- ◆ Problem Solving and Mathematical Reasoning
- ◆ Mathematical Skills and Tools
- ◆ Mathematical Communication.

Directions to the Student

Maria is going to visit her cousins for the weekend. For pants, she packs a pair of purple pants, a pair of jeans, and a pair of blue shorts. For tops, she takes a blue tee-shirt, a white tank top, a yellow blouse, and a green shirt. In addition, she has three pairs of socks: white, yellow, and blue. How many different outfits can she make? (An outfit consists of a pair of pants, a top, and a matching pair of socks.)

A picture or table will help you to organize the information.

Write a description of how you figured out your answer.

About This Task

This task involves different combinations of a set of clothing each of which makes a different outfit. Since Maria has a given number of tops, pants, and socks, her outfits may be listed and counted. The challenge for the student is to use a systematic approach that will ensure that all the possibilities have been considered.

Note: for some students, considering only tops and pants is a sufficient challenge. If desired, the task may be simplified in this manner.

Solution

If the tops are assigned capital letters (A, B, C, and D), the pants or shorts are assigned numbers (1, 2, and 3), and the socks are assigned small letters (a, b, and c), the outfits may be enumerated as A1a, A1b, A1c, A1a, A1b, A2c, A3a, A3b, A3c, B1a, B1b, B1c, B2a, B2b, B2c, B3a, B3b, B3c, C1a, C1b, C1c, C2a, C2b, C2c, C3a, C3b, C3c, and D1a, D1b, D1c, D2a, D2b, D2c, D3a, D3b, D3c. The total number of outfits is $4 \times 3 \times 3$, or 36.

Many students will make a diagram to illustrate the situation, such as the following:

Tops

Pants

Socks

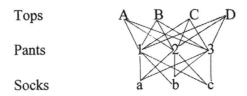

Alternatively, students might determine that for each top, there are 9 possible outfits. Since there are four different tops, the total number of possible outfits is 4 × 9, or 36.

Rubric

	Level One	**Level Two**	**Level Three**	**Level Four**
Problem Solving Approach	The student doesn't use a method or the method used is completely inappropriate.	The student uses an appropriate method, but does not fully execute it.	The student uses an appropriate method.	The student uses a method that is elegant and efficient, revealing comprehensive understanding.
Accuracy and Procedural Skill	Solution is unsupported.	Solution is accurate but the computations do not fully support the solution.	Solution is accurate, with minor computational errors.	Solution is accurate, and the calculations demonstrate understanding of the structure of the problem.
Communication	Description is completely missing or inadequate. The student randomly presents information.	Description conveys some aspects of the method the student used for solving the problem, but is incomplete. The student attempts to organize the information; however it is incomplete or leads to errors.	Description adequately conveys a systematic method for solving the problem. The student organizes information in a fairly systematic manner.	Description clearly conveys an elegant and efficient method for solving the problem. In addition, the explanation reveals an understanding of the patterns inherent in the situation, e.g., how to solve similar problems. The student organizes information in an efficient and systematic manner.

Samples of Student Work

Level One

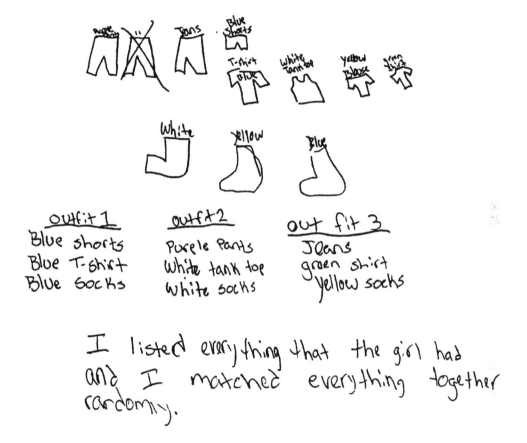

I listed everything that the girl had and I matched everything together randomly.

This response indicates no understanding of the concept of combinations, with three outfits formed randomly.

130 ◆ Middle School Mathematics Performance Tasks

Level One

In this response the student has applied a totally incorrect procedure, namely that of raising 2 to the power of 10. This student apparently recognizes that *something* must be done to the numbers to determine the combinations, and so applies an exotic approach.

Level Two

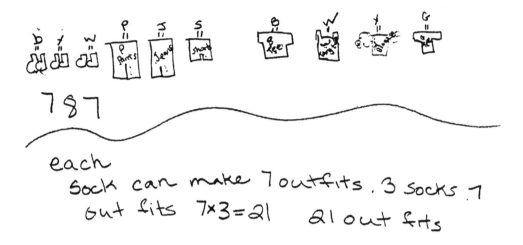

This response is a weak Level Two because, while the student apparently recognizes the need for a systematic approach to solve the problem, the system itself is seriously flawed. The statement that "each sock can make 7 outfits" was presumably made because there are four tops and three types of pants, and that 4 + 3 = 7. This is incorrect: each pair of socks can be used to make 12 different outfits (4 × 3 = 12). However, the solution is not a random one, and reflects the recognition of a pattern.

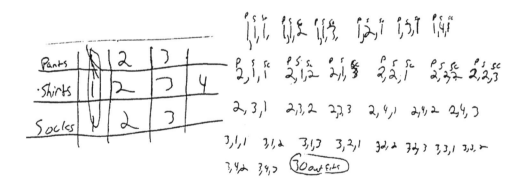

This response is a solid Level Two, with a reasonable approach to organizing the information. However, the student did not follow through with the system, resulting in an incorrect answer.

Level Three

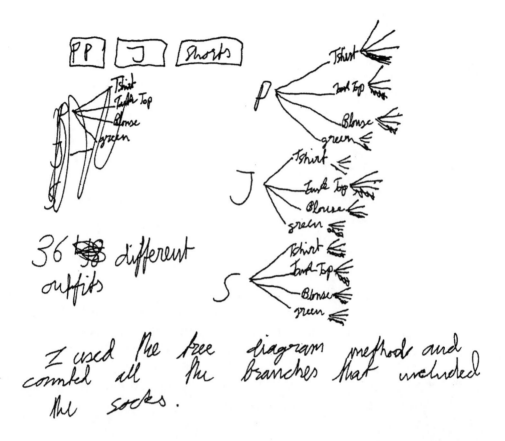

This response represents an accurate diagram of the situation, and by counting, an accurate solution. However, the presentation is organized in a fairly systematic manner but the explanation is not fully elaborated.

Level Three

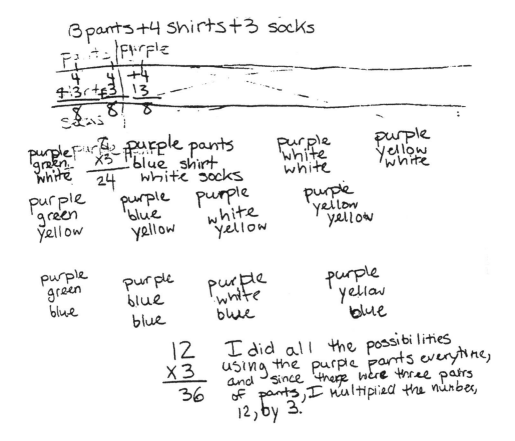

In this response the student enumerated all the possibilities for the purple pants and then multiplied the answer by 3. The system is not highly efficient or elegant; had it been, the solution would have been a Level Four.

134 ◆ Middle School Mathematics Performance Tasks

Level Four

(♪♪)++++,♪♪♪

PP, J, BS, B, W YB, GS, WS, YS, BSO
AP BP CP   AS BS CS DS

Key

AP = Purple Pants
BP = Jeans
CP = blue shorts

AS = blue tee-shirt
BS = white tank top
CS = yellow blouse
DS = green shirt

NS = white socks
YS = Yellow socks
BSO Blue socks

I made a chart that showed the possible outfits that can be made from Mama's vacationing wardrobe. I put the pairs of pants on the Y axis and the shirts on the x axis. I then added 3 pairs of sox to each combination box and counted up to reach my answer.

In this response the student clearly understands the need for a systematic approach to the problem, and an organized structure to the data. The use of symbols for the different types of clothing is highly efficient, and the description of the procedure used reveals a clear understanding of the problem and its solution.

Level Four

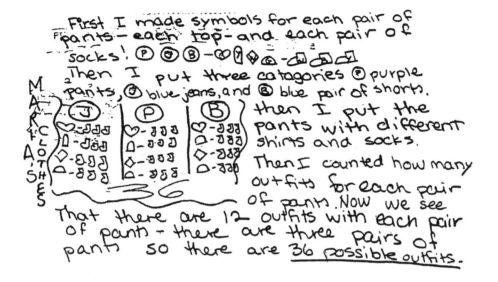

This response also demonstrates a clear understanding of the structure of the problem and the type of organization needed to solve it successfully. The approach is well designed, and the symbols are clear, yielding an accurate solution.

PIZZA PARTY

Mathematics Assessed

- ◆ Number Operations and Concepts
- ◆ Geometry and Measurement
- ◆ Functions and Algebra
- ◆ Problem Solving and Mathematical Reasoning
- ◆ Mathematical Skills and Tools
- ◆ Mathematical Communication.

Directions to the Student

Your class has decided to have pizza for its end-of-the-year party. You are trying to decide which pizza store has the cheapest price. The local pizza stores and their prices are listed below.

Pizza Prices

Sam's Pizza House	$8.50, 8 slices per pizza
Pizza Palace	$10.25, 10 slices per pizza
Pizza & Stuff	$6.25, 6 slices per pizza

Assume that there are 30 students in your class and that each person (including your teacher) will eat two slices. Also, assume that the slices of pizza from the different stores contain the same amount of pizza. Where should you buy the pizza?

Show all your work and write a brief description of how you decided on your answer.

About This Task

This task requires students to determine the best value for pizza. In this case they must consider both the number of pizzas needed from each source and the unit price per slice.

Solution

- Sam's Pizza House offers pizza at $8.50 for 8 slices. That comes to $1.06 per slice.
- Pizza Palace offers pizza at $10.25 for 10 slices. That comes to $1.02 per slice.
- Pizza & Stuff offers pizza at $6.25 for 6 slices. That comes to $1.04 per slice.

From this analysis it appears that Pizza Palace is the cheapest source of pizza. However, we must also consider the number of pizzas that must be purchased for each person to have two slices.

The class and the students together will eat 62 slices of pizza. That means they would have to buy:

8 pizzas from Sam's Pizza House for $68.00

7 pizzas from Pizza Palace for $71.75

11 pizzas from Pizza & Stuff for $68.75.

Thus, it appears that the cheapest source of pizza, considering the number of pizzas that must be purchased, is Sam's Pizza House.

Rubric

	Level One	Level Two	Level Three	Level Four
Problem Solving Approach	The student doesn't use a method or the method used is completely inappropriate.	The student uses an appropriate method, but does not fully execute it.	The student uses an appropriate method.	The student uses a method that is elegant and efficient, revealing comprehensive understanding.
Accuracy and Procedural Skill	Solution is unsupported.	Solution is accurate but the computations do not fully support the solution.	Solution is accurate, with minor computational errors.	Solution is accurate, and the calculations demonstrate understanding of the structure of the problem.

(continued)

(continued)

	Level One	Level Two	Level Three	Level Four
Communication	Description is completely missing or inadequate. The student randomly presents information.	Description conveys some aspects of the method the student used for solving the problem, but is incomplete. The student attempts to organize the information; however it is incomplete or leads to errors.	Description adequately conveys a systematic method for solving the problem. The student organizes information in a fairly systematic manner.	Description clearly conveys an elegant and efficient method for solving the problem. In addition, the explanation reveals an understanding of the patterns inherent in the situation, e.g., how to solve similar problems. The student organizes information in an efficient and systematic manner.

Middle School Mathematics Performance Tasks ◆ 139

PLANNING A PLAYGROUND

Mathematics Assessed

- ◆ Number Operations and Concepts
- ◆ Geometry and Measurement
- ◆ Functions and Algebra
- ◆ Problem Solving and Mathematical Reasoning
- ◆ Mathematical Skills and Tools
- ◆ Mathematical Communication.

Directions to the Student

You have been hired by a town's recreation department to fence in an area to be used for a playground. You have been provided with 60 feet of fencing (in 4-foot sections), and a 4-foot gate. How can you put up the fence so that children have the maximum amount of space in which to play?

Try several different shapes that can be made with the fencing and calculate their areas. Include pictures of these shapes, drawing them roughly to scale. In addition, write a brief summary that describes which shape you think will have the largest area and why.

For an additional challenge, imagine that the fencing is flexible, and can be made to bend. What shape would have the greatest area and why?

About This Task

This task concerns the relationship of area and perimeter. For a given perimeter, as the shape enclosed approximates a circle, the area increases. For example, a playground shaped like a skinny rectangle would use a lot of fencing for a small area. If the same amount of fencing were used to enclose a playground in the shape of a square, the area would be larger, and if it were used to enclose the shape of a regular octagon, the area would be larger still. Moreover, a circle would produce the largest area for the given amount of fencing.

Solution

The amount of fencing, including the 4-foot gate, is 64 feet. Since it is in 4-foot sections, the only rectangles that can be made with it are:

140 ◆ Middle School Mathematics Performance Tasks

28′ × 4′ with an area of 112 square feet

24′ × 8′ with an area of 192 square feet

20′ × 12′ with an area of 240 square feet

16′ × 16′ with an area of 256 square feet.

A circle, on the other hand, made with the same amount of fencing, contains much more area. The formula for the relationship between the circumference and the diameter (or radius) is $C = \pi D$ or $C = 2\pi r$. Therefore, the radius = the circumference divided by 2 × pi, or 64 divided by about 2 × 3.14. The radius then is about 10.2 feet.

The formula for the area of a circle is $a = \pi r^2$. With a radius of 10.2 feet, the area of a circle made with the fencing is 327 square feet.

A regular octagon produces an area intermediate between that of a square and a circle, about 309 square feet. And if the fencing were made into other shapes, as the number of sides increases, approaching the shape of a circle, the area increases.

Rubric

	Level One	Level Two	Level Three	Level Four
Problem Solving Approach	Approach is random; only one solution found.	Approach is not very systematic, but several shapes are compared.	Approach is systematic.	Approach is highly systematic and reveals comprehensive understanding.
Accuracy and Procedural Skill	Many computational errors.	A number of computational errors and/ or formulae improperly applied.	Very few computational errors; formulae correctly applied.	Solution is accurate, and the calculations demonstrate understanding of the structure of the problem.
Communication	Drawing is unclear and erred. Little to no recognition of the effect of changing the number and lengths of sides on the area of a polygon.	Drawing is mostly clear; some errors in scale and/or labeling. There is some recognition of the effect of changing number and lengths of sides on the area of a polygon.	Drawing is labeled with the correct scale. The effect of changing the number of sides and length of sides on the area of a polygon is mostly understood. Explanation is clearly written.	Drawing is well represented revealing understanding of the relationship between number of sides, lengths of sides, and area of a polygon.

Samples of Student Work

Level One

I believe that #2 would provide the most space for the children to play. I think this is because it is wider than #1 and it is almost as long. It would use the same amount of fencing but have more ~~area~~ area space.

This response offers no measurements nor calculations of area; the conclusion is the result of an "eye-ball" guess only. It does not appear that the student has fully understood the question.

Level One

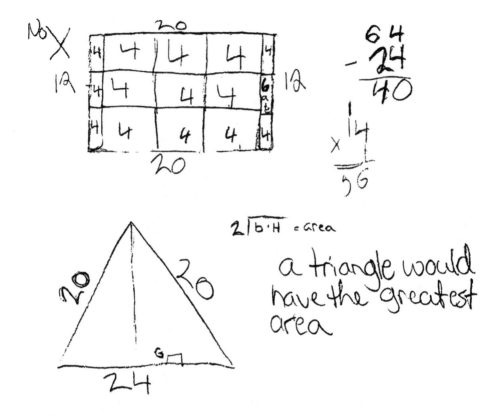

The student who submitted this response appears to be confused over the distinction between area and perimeter. While the dimensions of the rectangle and the triangle both measure 64 feet, their areas are not calculated correctly. Moreover, no other quadrilaterals are attempted (whose areas the student could probably determine) as a basis for comparison and for observing patterns.

Level Two

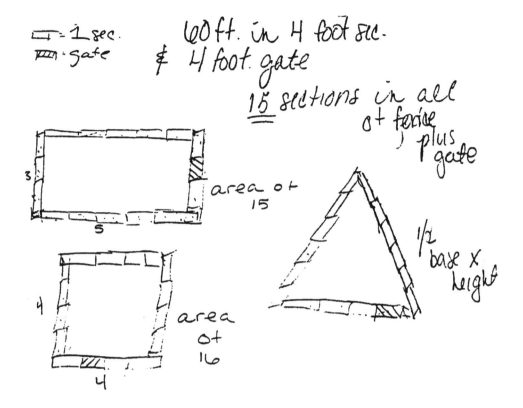

In this response, several shapes are compared as to their area. However, no conclusion is drawn, nor is an explanation provided.

Level Two

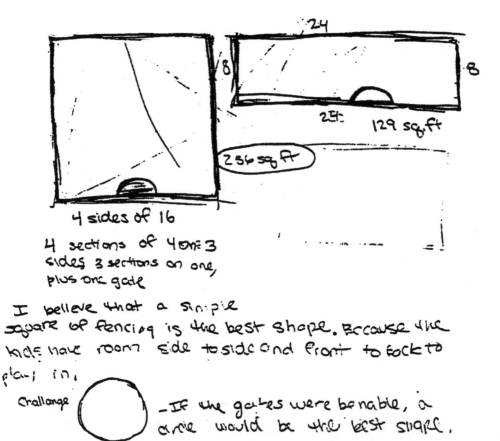

This is a Level Two plus response but not yet at Level Three. It contains an arithmetic or copying error, in that the area of one shape is noted as "129" rather than "192 square feet." The correct conclusion is given, but with no rationale. The rectangular drawings are clear and roughly to scale, and the answers are given in the proper units.

Level Three

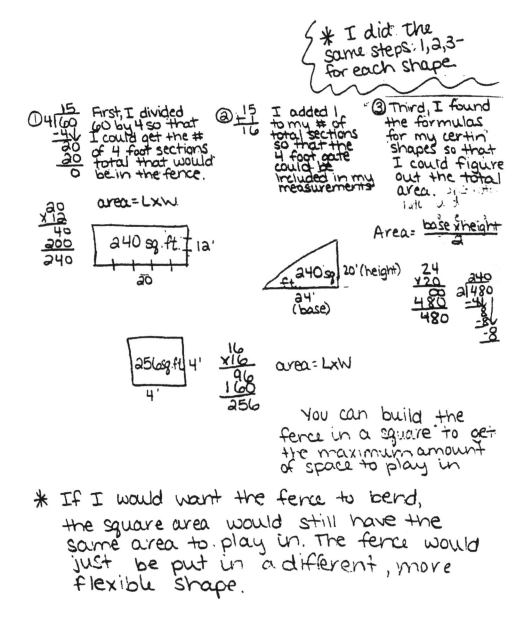

This response is a solid Level Three. It provides a very clear explanation and correct conclusion for the square, and accurate calculations for the several shapes explored. However, the extension to flexible fencing was not made correctly.

Level Three

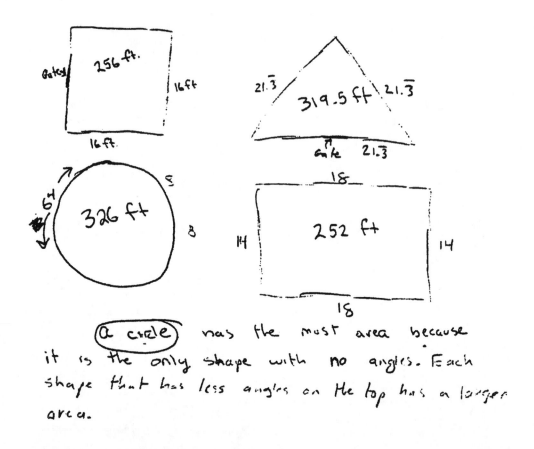

a circle has the most area because it is the only shape with no angles. Each shape that has less angles on the top has a larger area.

This response arrives at the correct answer and concludes that the circle is the shape with the largest area for its perimeter. However, the reason given (that "each shape that has less angles on the top has a larger area") is not accurate, and suggests less than complete understanding.

Level Four

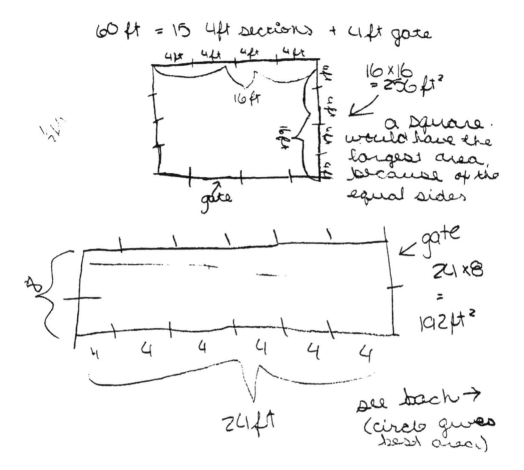

This response can be best evaluated as demonstrating the borderline between Level Three and Level Four. The student appears to understand the general principle that the closer a shape approaches a circle, the larger its area will be. However, the explanation is not very clear, nor is the presentation neat. The circle is not at all to scale.

Level Four (continued)

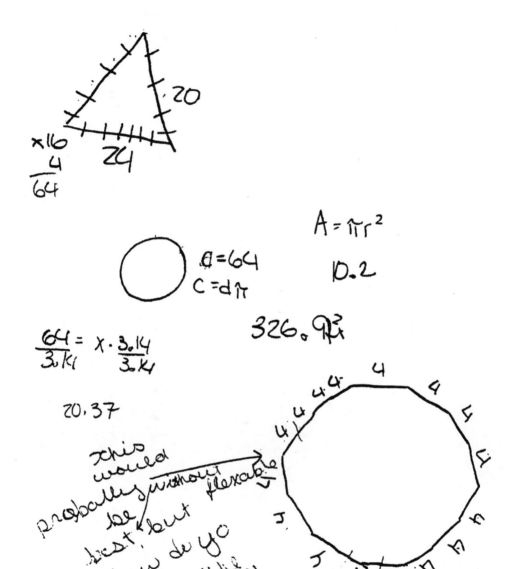

Level Four

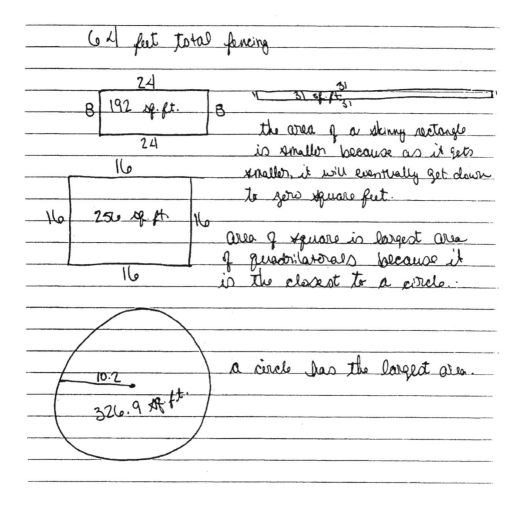

This response is an example of a clear Level Four on this task. The student not only arrives at the correct answer, but demonstrates understanding of the underlying mathematical principle, namely, that as shapes approach a circle their area increases and, conversely, that as rectangles become thinner and thinner (approaching a line) their area decreases to zero.

150 ◆ Middle School Mathematics Performance Tasks

POOL PLEASURE

Mathematics Assessed

- ◆ Number Operations and Concepts
- ◆ Geometry and Measurement
- ◆ Functions and Algebra
- ◆ Problem Solving and Mathematical Reasoning
- ◆ Mathematical Skills and Tools
- ◆ Mathematical Communication.

Directions to the Student

The Department of Recreation has obtained approval for the construction of a swimming pool and has requested your help with the design. The department would also like you to determine how much time it will take to fill the pool when it is built.

The pool will have to be able to hold at least 100 people and, in order for it not to be too crowded, you should allow 20 square feet of surface area per swimmer. The pool should be 3 feet deep in the shallow end and 9 feet deep in the deep end. You can make the shallow end as large as you like.

What are some possible shapes for the pool? Which do you like best?

When the pool is built, how long will it take to fill? If the Recreation Department wants to open the pool on May 25, when should they begin filling it? The pipe they will be using can supply water at the rate of 6 gallons per minute, and a cubic foot of water contains 7.48 gallons.

Draw a picture of your pool and write a letter to the Director of Recreation to explain your recommendations.

About This Task

This task requires that students determine the minimum area needed for the pool and possible dimensions to attain that area. They must also determine how much space to allow for the shallow end and the total volume contained by their design. Lastly, students must determine the time required for filling the pool, by converting rates of fill into hours and days needed.

Solution

Solutions will vary, depending on the pool shape selected by the student. However, a possible solution follows:

A pool which will allow 20 square feet for each of 100 people must have at least 2,000 square feet. One way to have that is with a pool 40' × 50'. Two pictures of the pool, from a bird's eye view and from the side, are shown below:

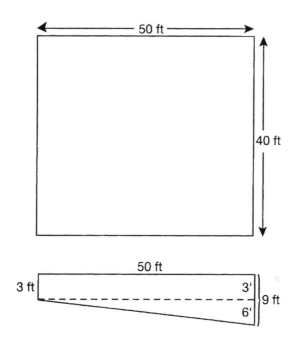

The volume of the pool is (3 × 40 × 50) + 6×50×40 / 2 cubic feet or 12,000 cubic feet 2.

At 7.48 gallons per cubic foot, there are 12,000 × 7.48 or 89,760 gallons in the pool.

To fill the pool with 89,760 gallons at 6 gallons per minute, 14,960 minutes are needed.

14,960 / 60 = 249.3 hours, or 10.4 days.

Therefore, the city should start filling the pool at least by May 14.

152 ◆ Middle School Mathematics Performance Tasks

Rubric

	Level One	Level Two	Level Three	Level Four
Problem Solving Approach	The student doesn't use a method or the method used is completely inappropriate.	The student uses an appropriate method, but does not fully execute it.	The student uses an appropriate method.	The student uses a method that is elegant and efficient, revealing comprehensive understanding.
Accuracy and Procedural Skill	Solution is unsupported.	Solution is accurate but the computations do not fully support the solution.	Solution is accurate, with minor computational errors.	Solution is accurate, and the calculations demonstrate understanding of the structure of the problem.
Communication	Description is completely missing or inadequate. Drawing of pool is inadequate and drawn without representation of scale. The student randomly presents information.	Description conveys some aspects of the method the student used for solving the problem, but is incomplete. The drawing of the pool is not entirely clear. The student attempts to organize the information; however it is incomplete or leads to errors.	Description adequately conveys a systematic method for solving the problem. The drawing of the pool shows one view and is mostly clear as to shape and scale. The student organizes information in a fairly systematic manner.	Description clearly conveys an elegant and efficient method for solving the problem. The drawing of the pool shows two views with a clear sense of scale. In addition, the explanation reveals an understanding of the patterns inherent in the situation, e.g., how to solve similar problems. The student organizes information in an efficient and systematic manner.

Middle School Mathematics Performance Tasks ◆ 153

POPCORN ESTIMATION

Mathematics Assessed

- ◆ Number Operations and Concepts
- ◆ Problem Solving and Mathematical Reasoning
- ◆ Mathematical Skills and Tools
- ◆ Mathematical Communication.

Directions to the Student

Estimate how many pieces of popcorn there are in the container. You may use any of the materials in the classroom, including graph paper, scales, cups, rulers, and calculators.

Explain your strategy and your reasoning. Think how you might verify your estimate.

Materials Needed

- ◆ A large jar filled with popcorn kernels
- ◆ Cups of several different sizes, such as portion cups from a hospital, 7 oz. cold drink cups
- ◆ Scales or pan balance and weights (standard or non-standard)
- ◆ Graph paper
- ◆ Calculators.

About This Task

This task requires that students devise a plan to estimate large numbers. It poses a challenge because the first response of most students—to simply count the kernels—is quickly discovered to be impossibly tedious. Therefore, students must create a strategy based on either area, volume, weight, or the successive dividing of numbers.

Solution

Solutions will vary, depending on the size and capacity of the container chosen for the popcorn. In addition, student approaches will also vary considerably, and could include any of the following:

- Counting the number of kernels in a small cup, finding out how many small cups fit into a larger cup and multiplying the number of large cups filled by the number of kernels.
- Weighing a sample of kernels (subtracting the weight of the cup if appropriate), weighing the total number of kernels and dividing to discover how many cups of kernels are present in the total and multiplying that number by the number of kernels in one cup.
- Counting the number of kernels that covers a square unit of graph paper and multiplying that number by the total number of squares covered by all the kernels.
- Dividing the kernels in halves, quarters, eighths, etc., until a number small enough to count easily is achieved, and then reversing the process.

Because of the many different approaches to this problem, it is an excellent vehicle for exploring different strategies and comparing their relative merits. Do they yield the same solutions? Is one approach likely to be more accurate than another?

Note: This task is adapted from one developed by Marge Petit, when she was a middle school teacher at Cabot School, Cabot, Vermont, and published by *Exemplars*, RR 1, P.O. Box 7390, Underhill, VT 05489.

Rubric

	Level One	Level Two	Level Three	Level Four
Problem Solving Approach	Random and disorganized; no systematic approach.	Some system is apparent in the approach, but it is not well organized.	Systematic and organized single approach.	Highly systematic and organized approach, verified through another approach.

Accuracy and Procedural Skill	Solution is missing or reasonable without supporting work.	Solution is attempted but reasonableness is not considered.	Solution is reasonable and mostly supported by work.	Solution is reasonable and fully supported by work.
Explanation	Little or no explanation is given.	Explanation is attempted, but difficult to understand.	Explanation is fairly clear, but the thinking process is not always easy to follow.	Explanation is very clear, and the thinking process is easy to follow.

156 ◆ Middle School Mathematics Performance Tasks

Samples of Student Work

Level One

the lady
put the popcorn in a
scale with cups. and then we
put some stuff in the other
side we did it because we
thought it would work and it
did. but first we were doing
somthing els with the popcorn
we were puting it on a ruler
then we stoped that. ~~and we~~
~~start it an~~

~~we did not~~
we used the skail
to hold it.

This response reveals little or no understanding of the problem nor a systematic approach to solving it.

Middle School Mathematics Performance Tasks ◆ 157

Level One

We had a scale
and som wates and
popcorn crnls. We
tuck a 5 gm and
put it on one
side and then
we put the pop
corn crnls in on
the other side and
wade it till it
was perfict. Then
we made little
pills and counted
them. They all
ecwold up to
55.

This response, while stronger than the previous example, demonstrates no coherent approach to the problem. The student appears to be still at the stage in the problem of exploring with the materials.

Level Two

The problem was to estimate How
many popcorn Kernels there were
in the container. We had these items
to help us figure out or estimate!
a Scale three sizes of Cups; a calculater;
a ruler; and some graph paper,

at frist we did not Know what to
do the we decided to make some
measurements to help us whith the
actual estimate. We figured out that
1 tile weighed the same as 50 popcorn
Kernels. based on that we did our
frist estimation we Just multiplied
52 × 52 becase that Looks good
up there ↗ our answer was 2074
wich Later became a very good
answer for we had two other
estimates within 400 of it, but
the other one was a bit high.

The way we got it was by
Counting the amount of kernels there
were in one midixm cup wich was 256
then we multipled the number
of cups there were in the container
wich was twelve our answer was 3072
a little higher than the other three estimates.

This response demonstrates understanding of the problem and appears to have been based on three different approaches to the problem. However, the explanation is difficult to follow and the computations are not clearly described.

Middle School Mathematics Performance Tasks ◆ 159

Level Three

We have another problem in Math in class. We have to estimate how many Popcorn kernels are in a big container by using tiny cups, big cups, weight scale, and a calculator

The first way we thought of to solve the problem was to pour the Popcorn into the scale so that there's exactly half in each side then we would count half, That way would take forever, so we found another way. Here's how we did it, We counted how many kernels fit in a little cup, exactly 246. Then we counted how little cups fit into big cups, 6. We had four big cups and 1 and a half little filled with Popcorn kernels. Then we multiplied 246 by 24 plus the extra popcorn and came up with our estimation of 6261. kernels. When I really think about it. The first way I tried to solve the problem wouldn't of taken so long if I devided the kernels into fourths and counted them I could have solved the problem two ways.

This response demonstrates a systematic approach to the problem and contains the hint of a second method that could have been used for verification. The explanation is clear and the computations are accurate and reasonable.

Level Four

The problem is to estimate how many popcorn kernels there are in a big container.

I wasn't quite sure if I was going to like this problem. In the end it turned out to be an okay problem.

How we figured it out was like this: We decided that we should figure out how many kernels would fit in a small cup. Because then we would be able to say when we filled up a small cup there are about so many kernels in this cup. There were 243 kernels.

So we filled the small cups then put the kernels into a bigger cup. Three of the small cups fit in the big cups.

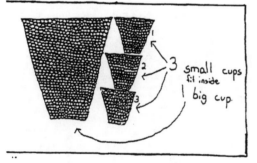

So we punched 243 into the calculator each time we filled a tiny cup. But in the end we ended up with 532,170 popcorn kernels! We knew that sounded kind of wrong so we decided to check our answer. We knew that three of the little cups filled with popcorn kernels fit

Middle School Mathematics Performance Tasks ◆ 161

Level Four (continued)

into one big cup. There were five big cups and one little cup so there were 16 little cups total. (see last page) Then we took the calculater and pressed in 16×243. The answer came out to be 3,888. So my group had two totally different answers. We didn't know which one was right! We decided to check one more time. This time we wrote 243 16 times on a peice of paper. When we added it all up it was 3,888.

So our final answer is 3,888.

Out of this problem I learned that the next time I use a calculater I need to be very careful that I press the numbers I want so I don't end up with a totally wild answer!

I will use estimation in my job when I grow up. Lets say I became an artest. I would estimate how much paint I would need to finish that picture and I would estimate how long it would take me to finish the picture.

The explanation in this solution is clear and easy to follow. Its author has a keen sense of the reasonableness of results, and the group had to re-do one of their estimates because of wildly different results. However, the response is a weak Level Four because it demonstrates essentially only one approach to the problem.

SKYDIVING

Mathematics Assessed

- ◆ Geometry and Measurement
- ◆ Problem Solving and Mathematical Reasoning
- ◆ Mathematical Skills and Tools
- ◆ Mathematical Communication.

Directions to the Student

Ms. Stewart (a teacher in the school) is planning to go skydiving. She wants to surprise Ms. Bucci and land on her farm. However, she would prefer to land on open area rather than on a building or in the pond. The area of Ms. Bucci's farm is about 5 acres or 220,000 square feet.

Using the aerial photograph of the farm in the space below, determine the probability that Miss Stewart will land in part of the open area of the farm.

Explain in words how you arrived at your answer.

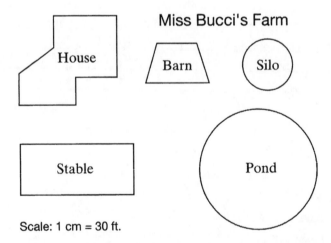

About This Task

This task requires that students apply skills of measurement and calculation to a semi-authentic situation. They must measure correctly, calculate areas of different shapes, and then calculate the percentage of land covered by the buildings and the pond and subtract from 100 percent.

Solution

Answers will vary depending on the size of the images on the photocopies given to students.

Rubric

	Level One	Level Two	Level Three	Level Four
Problem Solving Approach	Approach is random and disorganized, not systematic.	Approach reveals some system; however, it is difficult to follow.	Approach is systematic and organized, but not well presented.	Approach is highly systematic and organized; neatly and clearly presented.
Accuracy and Procedural Skill	Inappropriate operation(s) selected, and/or many errors, leading to wildly erroneous conclusions.	Mixture of appropriate and inappropriate operation ((s); some errors, but allowing largely for accurate conclusions.	Appropriate operation(s) selected; virtually no mathematical errors; with accurate conclusions.	The work is appropriate and contains no errors; in addition, the work shows evidence of advanced planning.
Communication	Explanation is lacking or is impossible to follow.	Explanation is attempted but is difficult to understand.	Explanation is fairly clear, but the thinking process is not always easy to follow.	Explanation is very clear, and the thinking process is easy to follow.

Note: This task was developed by Donna Bucci, eighth grade teacher in the Penn Delco School District, Ashton, PA.

164 ◆ Middle School Mathematics Performance Tasks

SPOT

Mathematics Assessed

- ◆ Number Operations and Concepts
- ◆ Functions and Algebra
- ◆ Problem Solving and Mathematical Reasoning
- ◆ Mathematical Skills and Tools
- ◆ Mathematical Communication.

Directions to the Student

Each month John weighs his puppy Spot, with the results shown below. If the pattern of the puppy's weight gain continues, how much will he weigh at 5 months? How much do you think Spot will weigh when he is fully grown?

Explain how you arrived at your answers.

Spot's Age	Spot's Weight
1 month	10 lb.
2 months	15 lb.
3 months	19 lb.
4 months	22 lb.
5 Months	?

About This Task

In this task, students must analyze the data provided to determine the pattern shown there. They must then extrapolate to determine the age at which Spot will not gain more weight.

This task is adapted from one developed for the National Assessment of Educational Progress (NAEP).

Middle School Mathematics Performance Tasks ◆ 165

Solution

This task, unlike many performance tasks, has a single right answer. The pattern in the weight gain is a gain of one less pound per month. That is, between months one and two, Spot gained 5 pounds, but only 4 pounds between months two and three, and 3 pounds between months three and four.

The pattern is illustrated in the table below:

Spot's Age	Spot's Weight	Weight Gain
1 month	10 lb.	–
2 months	15 lb.	5 lb.
3 months	19 lb.	4 lb.
4 months	22 lb.	3 lb.
5 months	24 lb.	2 lb.
6 months	25 lb.	1 lb.
7 months	25 lb.	0 lb.

Continuing the pattern, Spot would gain 2 pounds between months four and five, weighing 24 pounds at five months. Then, Spot would gain 1 additional pound between months five and six, but then gain no more weight. Therefore, he would have gained all his weight by the time he is six months old.

Rubric

	Level One	Level Two	Level Three	Level Four
Problem Solving Approach	No recognition of the pattern.	Recognition that there is a pattern, but incorrect conclusion as to what it is.	Correct recognition of pattern but inability to extend.	Correct recognition and extension of pattern.

(continued)

(continued)

	Level One	Level Two	Level Three	Level Four
Accuracy and Procedural Skill	Solution is unsupported.	Solution is accurate but the computations do not fully support the solution.	Solution is accurate, with minor computational errors.	Solution is accurate, and the calculations demonstrate understanding of the structure of the problem.
Communication	Explanation is not provided or is wholly inadequate.	Explanation is unclear.	Explanation is clear.	Explanation is very clear and well-articulated.

Middle School Mathematics Performance Tasks ◆ 167

TRAFFIC LIGHTS

Mathematics Assessed

- ◆ Statistics and Probability
- ◆ Problem Solving and Mathematical Reasoning
- ◆ Mathematical Skills and Tools
- ◆ Mathematical Communication.

Directions to the Student

It often seems as though traffic lights are always red! Sometimes, though, you can be lucky, and ride through a whole series of lights that turn green just as you approach them.

Imagine you are on a bus, riding along a stretch of road with five traffic lights and that the probability of the light being red when the bus gets to an intersection is 50%. What is the probability that all the lights will be red when your bus gets to them? What is the probability that they will all be green? (For the purpose of this problem, assume that an amber light is the same as a green light.)

Write an explanation of how you arrived at your answer.

About This Task

This task requires students to apply concepts of probability to a practical situation they are likely to encounter frequently.

Solution

This problem, unlike many performance tasks, has a single correct answer.

Since the probability of any one light being red (or green) is 50%, the likelihood of all the lights being red (or green) when a person reaches them is $1/2 \times 1/2 \times 1/2 \times 1/2 \times 1/2$ or 1/32, or about 3%.

Some students might try to solve the problem by adding the probabilities of each of the individual events, rather than multiplying them.

Rubric

	Level One	Level Two	Level Three	Level Four
Problem Solving Approach	The student doesn't use a method or the method used is completely inappropriate.	The student uses an appropriate method, but does not fully execute it.	The student uses an appropriate method.	The student uses a method that is elegant and efficient, revealing comprehensive understanding.
Accuracy and Procedural Skill	Solution is unsupported.	Solution is accurate but the computations do not fully support the solution.	Solution is accurate, with minor computational errors.	Solution is accurate, and the calculations demonstrate understanding of the structure of the problem.
Communication	Description is completely missing or inadequate. The student randomly presents information.	Description conveys some aspects of the method the student used for solving the problem, but is incomplete. The student attempts to organize the information; however it is incomplete or leads to errors.	Description adequately conveys a systematic method for solving the problem. The student organizes information in a fairly systematic manner.	Description clearly conveys an elegant and efficient method for solving the problem. In addition, the explanation reveals an understanding of the patterns inherent in the situation, e.g., how to solve similar problems. The student organizes information in an efficient and systematic manner.

Middle School Mathematics Performance Tasks ◆ 169

UNICYCLE RACES

Mathematics Assessed

- ◆ Function and Algebra Concepts
- ◆ Number and Operations Concepts
- ◆ Problem Solving and Mathematical Reasoning
- ◆ Mathematical Skills and Tools
- ◆ Mathematical Communication.

About This Task

In this task, students use rates and distance to determine the time it takes to complete a race and the type of unicycle necessary to go a given distance in a given amount of time. Students find an average speed given three different rates and times.

Directions to the Student

Katie and Brian are going to ride in a 30 mile unicycle race.

Katie is in the small unicycle category, riding a 20 inch unicycle that, according to the manufacturer, averages about 5 mph in races but can reach a maximum speed of 8 mph.

Brian is in the midsize unicycle category, riding a 29 inch unicycle that, according to the manufacturer, averages about 7 mph in races but can reach a maximum speed of 14 mph.

- a. Katie thinks that she might complete the race in less time than Brian completes the race. Brian says that is impossible. What do you think? Explain.
- b. Their friend, Ambra, is entered in the large unicycle category, riding a 36-inch unicycle that, according to the manufacturer, averages about 11 mph in races but can reach a maximum speed of 22 mph. If she rides at 22 mph for 1/4 of the race, 15 mph for 1/4 of the race, and 8 mph for 1/2 of the race, what is Ambra's average speed? How long does it take her to finish the race? Show the work that led to your answers.
- c. A unicycle rider set a record for riding 282 miles in 24 hours. What size unicycle do you think he might have ridden? Explain.

170 ◆ Middle School Mathematics Performance Tasks

Solution

a. Sample solution: *It is possible for Katie to complete the race in less time than Brian as long as her average speed is more than his average speed over the course of the race. For example, if she averaged 7 mph and he averaged 6 mph, she would finish the race in less time than Brian. However, if he rode at the average speed of 7 mph given for his unicycle, she would have to ride close to the maximum speed of her unicycle, 8 mph, which would be very difficult. So, I think it is unlikely that she will complete the course in less time than Brian.*

b. Ambra's average speed was 13 1/4 mph since 22 (1/4) + 15 (1/4) + 8 (1/2) =13 1/4 mph. At that speed, if took Ambra about 2 1/4 hours since 30/(13 1/4) is about 2.26.

c. I think he might have ridden a large unicycle like the one Ambra rode since 282 miles/24 hours = 11.75 mph, which is close to the average speed of a 36-inch unicycle as given by the manufacturer.

Rubric

	Level One	**Level Two**	**Level Three**	**Level Four**
Problem Solving Approach	Method used to find the time or rate is disorganized, with no evidence of the relationship between distance, rate and time.	Method used to find time or rate reveals some attempt at consistency, but not completely carried through.	Method used to find time or rate is consistent, and if followed would yield correct solutions.	The method used to find time or rate is consistent and with evidence of complete understanding of the relationship between distance, rate and time.
Accuracy and Procedural Skill	Many errors in calculations, yielding wildly erroneous results.	Some computational inaccuracies, resulting in minor errors in the results.	Only minor errors in calculations; correct application of method.	No errors in computation; correct application of method.
Communication	Explanations and work are unclear and difficult to follow.	Explanations and work are coherent, but reveal imperfect understanding of the problem.	Explanations and work are clear and reflect understanding of most parts of the problem.	Explanations and work are clear and reflect understanding of all parts of the problem.

Middle School Mathematics Performance Tasks ◆ 171

VARIABLE DILEMMA

Mathematics Assessed

- ◆ Number Operations and Concepts
- ◆ Problem Solving and Mathematical Reasoning
- ◆ Mathematical Skills and Tools
- ◆ Mathematical Communication.

Directions to the Student

Each letter in the equations below stands for a different whole number (0–9). Look at each equation carefully. Think about what you know about how numbers work. Find the value of each letter (A–J).

Write a brief summary of how you found your answer. It need not describe every step, but should enable a reader to understand your approach.

1. $G + G + G = D$
2. $J + E = J$
3. $G^2 = D$
4. $B + G = D$
5. $F - B = C$
6. $I/H = A\ (H > A)$
7. $A \times C = A$.

About This Task

This task requires that students apply what they know about properties of numbers (such as the identity and zero principles of addition and multiplication) to solve the problem. In addition, they must be able to suspend judgment until they have sufficient information on which to reach a conclusion and try out different solutions. Lastly, they must be able to communicate their findings and the procedure they have used.

172 ◆ Middle School Mathematics Performance Tasks

Solution

The solution is:

A = 2   F = 7

B = 6   G = 3

C = 1   H = 4

D = 9   I = 8

E = 0   J = 5

A possible procedure is as follows:

- Equations #1 and #3 can be combined to conclude that G = 3 and D = 9.
- From equation #4 and the statement above it can be concluded that B = 6.
- From equation #2 we know that E = 0; J can be anything.
- From equation #7 we know that C = 1; A can be anything.
- From equation #5, since C = 1, F = 7.
- Using equation #6 and the numbers remaining, I = 8, H = 4 and A = 2.
- J must be 5, since it is the only number left, and J can be anything.

Note: This task is adapted from one developed by Anne Rainey in Shelburne, Vermont, with student work from Clare Forseth's class at the Marion Cross School in Norwich, Vermont, and published by *Exemplars*, RR 1, P.O. Box 7390, Underhill, VT 05489.

Rubric

	Level One	Level Two	Level Three	Level Four
Problem Solving Approach	The student doesn't use a method or the method used is completely inappropriate.	The student uses an appropriate method, but does not fully execute it.	The student uses an appropriate method.	The student uses a method that is elegant and efficient, revealing comprehensive understanding.

Accuracy and Procedural Skill	Solution is unsupported.	Solution is accurate but the computations do not fully support the solution.	Solution is accurate, with minor computational errors.	Solution is accurate, and the calculations demonstrate understanding of the structure of the problem.
Communication	Description is completely missing or inadequate. The student randomly presents information.	Description conveys some aspects of the method the student used for solving the problem, but is incomplete. The student attempts to organize the information; however it is incomplete or leads to errors.	Description adequately conveys a systematic method for solving the problem. The student organizes information in a fairly systematic manner.	Description clearly conveys an elegant and efficient method for solving the problem. In addition, the explanation reveals an understanding of the patterns inherent in the situation, e.g., how to solve similar problems. The student organizes information in an efficient and systematic manner.

174 ◆ Middle School Mathematics Performance Tasks

Samples of Student Work

Level One

1) First I looked at problem J+E=J. I counted up until I got to J. J is the tent., letter. So I wrote 10 under the J's. But the problem is addition. So far I had 10 + blank = 10. E must be 0, so that equals: 10+0=10.

2) The next problem I did was F-G=C. B =C, so. F-B=C 7-G=1.)

This response exhibits little awareness of a systematic approach to the problem and provides little explanation.

Level Two

$$6A = 4 \quad 6I = 2$$
$$4B = 6 \quad 7J = 7$$
$$1C = 1$$
$$4D = 9$$
$$2E = 0$$
$$5F = 5$$
$$3G = 3$$
$$7H - 8$$

The first letter I got was C which = 1 because any thing times 1 = the same number.

The second letter I got was E because anything +zero equals that mumber

The third letter I got was 6 the way I got it was I just had to fool around with other letters and number thats also how I got the two fourth letters

176 ◆ Middle School Mathematics Performance Tasks

The Fith letter I got was F the way I got it I just had too think about it

The sixth letters I were A,H,I the way I got them Were I looked and saw the numbers I had not used and then tried it and got the answers

The seventh letter I got was J because I forgot abbout it but then I saw that I had used all the numbers below 10 and 10+0 =10 and that was the answer.

This response offers a fairly complete explanation of the procedure followed. However, several of the findings are inaccurate, making others inaccurate also. Awareness of the identity properties of 0 and 1 permit this student to correctly conclude that C = 1 and E = 0. However, after that point the steps in reasoning break down, making successful solving of the problem impossible.

Middle School Mathematics Performance Tasks ◆ 177

Level Three

$$2 \times 1 = 2$$

C =1 because A × C = A and I solved first because any number × itself is one. I came up with A = 2 because I tried different numbers with different equations and A had to be 2. Then I did all the other equations and came up with this chart. A= 2 B =6 C = 1 D = 9 E = 0 F=7 G=3 H=4 I = 8 J= 5.

If the numbers didn't have to equal one through nine, than J could be any number because J only shows up on the paper in one equation and it could be <u>any</u> number. e.g. 20=J+0 = E = 2 = J

This response arrives at a correct solution to the problem, although the explanation is not complete. However, the student appears to understand the problem and applies the relevant principles of algebra correctly.

178 ◆ Middle School Mathematics Performance Tasks

Level Four

First I discored that $O=E$ because $J+E=J$ and I know that in addition any number plus zero is itself. So on my chart (preivos page) I put a check where E met zero and knowing O or E cooldn't be anything else I crossed out all the other possdoiltys for zero and E.

Then I saw $A \times C = A$ and I knew that any number times one is its self. So $C=1$.

Then I saw $G^2=D$ and $G+G+G=D$ so I listed all squares under ten $1, 4, 9$ then I thooght $\sqrt{1} \sqrt[2]{4} \sqrt[3]{9}$ then $1+1+1=3$ $2+2+2=6$ $3+3+3=9$, and I saw $3^2=9$ and $3+3+3=9$ so $G=3$ and $D=9$.

After knowing $3=G$ $D=9$ I saw $B+G=D$ and so I thought $B+3=9$ and figored $B=6$ because $6+3=9$.

Knowing $B=6$ and $C=1$ I saw $F-B=C$ or $F-6=1$ and relized $7-6=1$ $F=7$.

Then I saw $1-H=8$ ($H>A$). I thought A can't be 8 because it has to be less than H, and H can't be 2 because $H>A$. I also relized $I \neq H$ because you're diving I so H wasn't 8 and I wasn't 3. Then after I thoght for a bit. I_came up with $8+4=2$ it was the only possable combanation so $A=2$ $H=4$ and I eqoaled 8.

It was then that I saw J codd only be 5.

This problem remirds me of logic problems because if you set it up in a grid the same rules apply.

Level Four (continued)

The explanation in this solution is clear and easy to follow. Its author has developed a systematic procedure for keeping track of which numbers have been used. The approach is logical and systematic, yielding a correct solution with a minimum of trial and error.